ADVANCE PRAISE FOR
A LEADER'S GIFT

"Barry tells us about the importance of encouragement and describes what it means to care for those we lead. A powerful and positive message about how to earn the right to be followed."

—**Linda Fisher Thornton, CEO, Leading in Context, and author of** *7 Lenses: Learning the Principles and Practices of Ethical Leadership*

"I first met Barry at a National Speaker's Association conference and was immediately struck by his interest, encouragement, and caring for everyone he met. Later I learned of his amazing Leadership skills based on Giving rather than Getting, Influence rather than Authority, and Putting People First. He truly models the simple but life-changing principles in this powerful book. His honesty, transparency, and use of real life stories will touch your mind, heart, and spirit, and you will be transformed to become a better leader, parent, and friend. Both Barry and "The Leader's Gift" are truly gifts to our world!"

—**Barbara A. Glanz, CSP, CPAE, author of** *180 Ways to Spread Contagious Enthusiasm* **and** *Handle with CARE: Motivating and Retaining Employees*

"Barry's five simple steps reinforce the truth behind leadership: successful leaders give more than they take. *A Leader's Gift* can help you fundamentally change your leadership style to get the best out of your business, your employees, and yourself."

—**Melinda F. Emerson, SmallBizLady, and bestselling author of** *Become Your Own Boss in 12 Months*

"Easy-to-read, practical advice that helps you evaluate your leadership style and challenges you to do better by your company, your colleagues, and yourself."

—**Lesley Hanak, Vice President for Human Resources, Savannah College of Art and Design**

"This book is an easy but important read about leadership learned through vicariously living and being."
—**Richard Schubert, former President, American Red Cross**

"The principles of great leadership resonate no matter how many people you lead. Barry can help you empower your employees and earn their respect and loyalty, whether you lead five or five hundred."
—**Connie Dieken, bestselling author of *Become the Real Deal* and *Talk Less, Say More***

"Barry Banther courageously opens his heart and bares all so that we can become better leaders. Full of honest disclosure and lessons learned from a lifetime of leadership, *A Leader's Gift* is a treasure not to be missed. To provide outstanding service to customers, you must first provide that same service to your people. This book is full of immediately implementable ideas; not about parties, recognition pins, and plaques but the real behavior change needed to become a leader others will follow. Reading this book was a present I gave myself. It's one I encourage you to give yourself too."
—**Donna Cutting, author of *The Celebrity Experience: Insider Secrets to Delivering Red-Carpet Customer Service***

"*A Leader's Gift* forces self-reflection that is valuable no matter how many years you have been leading. Barry makes you answer the tough questions about yourself and how you lead. A must read for any leader!"
—**Coley Herrin, President, PDI**

"The correct words given will change a person's life. *A Leader's Gift* has the correct words on every page."
—**Mark Jones, President, Air Ambulance Worldwide, Inc.**

"*A Leader's Gift* is an incredible gift to all who want to lead well at work and at home. For 25 years, Barry Banther has generously poured the five transformational gifts of a lasting leader into my life, and the lives of countless others."
—**Mark Merrill, President of Family First, and author of *All Pro Dad***

"*A Leader's Gift* gives smart advice about being a leader that makes a difference. Barry makes you feel like you're getting coached by a friend, not an advisor."

—**Peter van Stralen, CEO, Sunshine Brands™, The Grounds Guys®, and The Sprinkler Guys®, and author of *C.A.R.E. Leadership***

"Barry shows that the bottom line isn't made up of numbers; it's made up of human potential. *A Leader's Gift* offers five actionable steps to help first-time leaders and C-suite executives tap that potential and get the best out of their employees. Implementing these simple changes every day will make a world of difference!"

—**Laura Stack, past President, National Speakers Association, and author of *Execution IS the Strategy***

"Barry shows you how to balance management and leadership, maintaining authority while gaining respect."

—**LeAnn Thieman author of *Balance Life in Your 'War Zones'* and 12 Chicken Soup for the Soul titles**

"A refreshing, humble approach to leadership. By emphasizing empowerment instead of control, *A Leader's Gift* stands out from the shelves of leadership books."

—**Dr. Marta Wilson, CEO, Transformation Systems, Inc., author of *Leaders in Motion and Energized Enterprise***

"Barry Banther had the traditional (masculine) form of leadership nailed. He transformed his leadership to include ways of being—openness, honoring others, listening, and connecting—that are more feminine in nature. His five qualities help us all become the more whole and effective leaders needed today."

—**Caroline Turner, author of *Difference Works: Improving Retention, Productivity and Profitability through Inclusion***

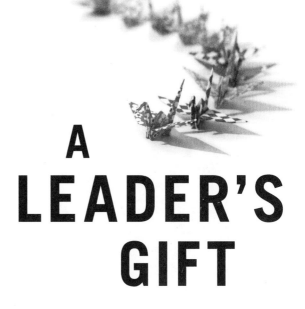

A
LEADER'S
GIFT

A LEADER'S GIFT

How to Earn the Right to Be Followed

. . .

BARRY BANTHER

GREENLEAF
BOOK GROUP PRESS

Published by Greenleaf Book Group Press
Austin, Texas
www.gbgpress.com

Distributed by Greenleaf Book Group LLC

For ordering information or special discounts for bulk purchases, please contact Greenleaf Book Group LLC at PO Box 91869, Austin, TX 78709, 512.891.6100.

Design and composition by Greenleaf Book Group LLC
Cover design by Greenleaf Book Group LLC
Image credits: Cover: ©iStockphoto.com/boboling;
Interior: [gift] ©iStockphoto.com/windujedi; [thank you note] ©iStockphoto.com/MrPlumo

Publisher's Cataloging-In-Publication Data

Banther, Barry.
  A leader's gift : how to earn the right to be followed / Barry Banther.—1st ed.
  p. ; cm.
  Issued also as an ebook.
  Includes bibliographical references.
  ISBN: 978-1-62634-056-5
  1. Leadership. 2. Employee empowerment. 3. Management. 4. Success in business. I. Title.
HD57.7 .B36 2014
658.4/092   2013945374

Part of the Tree Neutral® program, which offsets the number of trees consumed in the production and printing of this book by taking proactive steps, such as planting trees in direct proportion to the number of trees used: www.treeneutral.com

TreeNeutral®

Printed in the United States of America on acid-free paper

14 15 16 17 18 19   10 9 8 7 6 5 4 3 2 1

First Edition

This book is dedicated to my clients.
You have graciously invited me into your work life and, sometimes,
into your personal life, and mine has been the better for it.
I will always be grateful for you.

CONTENTS

· · · · · · · · · · · · · · · · · · · ·

ACKNOWLEDGMENTS

. . . .

This book is the result of decades of encouragement, support, and patience from dozens of people. Without their help my work would have failed long ago.

The first ones to thank are my family. Janice and I have been married for almost four decades, have raised two sons, and often have worked together in organizations. Throughout the good times and the difficult ones, she has always believed in me as a leader, and she urged me to complete this book. It would not have happened without her. I will always be thankful for her.

As I was finishing this manuscript, my oldest son, David, was in the middle of running in his first election—for city commissioner—and also managing our consulting firm, but he and his wife, Ruth, constantly found time to encourage me. My youngest son, John, and his fiancée, Zenas, were on an extended concert tour, yet every few days I would get an email asking me how it was going. And David and Ruth's three-year-old daughter, Miss Olivia, knows exactly how to reach her granddaddy's heart and inspire him. My family is a blessing to me.

My extended family also know how each of them has helped me both personally and professionally: Bobby and Bev Banther, Bob and Leah, Tara and Pepe, Ashley, Brian, LaWanda, Donna and Brett, Ryan, Sophia, Wanda, Keith, Shelley, and Ginger Morrell. All of you have helped me when I needed it most. I am blessed to have a family that loves me unconditionally.

Along with my family there are friends who have encouraged me in ways I am sure they don't realize. Some I have not seen in a long time, but that does not lessen the impact their friendship has had on my life and my growth as a leader. Dave and Becky Madasz, Mark and Susan Merrill, Mark and Sue Jones, Monde and Judy Flores, Lou and Anita Piniella, Ray and Nancy Murray, Dave and Vonna Furnish, Mike and Betsy Herd, Tom and Beth Goodgame, Howard and Judy Balm, Danny and Debby Miller, Mike and Carol Smith, Victor and Bev Costa, Jerry Foute, Frank Kennedy, Dr. Jim and Heather Gills, Glen and Marty Keys, Dr. Wayne Freeburg, C. Alex Roane (my first leadership coach), and one of my oldest friends, since we were classmates in elementary school, an exceptional teacher and encourager, Joyce Green.

I cannot thank my staff at Banther Consulting Corporation enough for their help. David and Ruth Banther, my business partners, along with Jackie Becker, Irene Wright, and David Difranco, are the rock our work is built on. I wouldn't be in business without them.

The most pleasant surprise in this project has been working with my development editor, Chris Benguhe, a highly accomplished journalist, writer, and editor. When Chris and I first discussed this work, I recognized his talent. What I grew to appreciate, however, is his ability to bring out the genuine life story that is in each of us. This book would never have happened without his coaching, both challenging and encouraging me at just the right moments.

Another person who was there at the right moment for me was a long-time colleague and friend, Fawn Germer. Fawn is an award-winning journalist and best-selling author who, over lunch one summer afternoon, simply said, "You have to write this now." Those words haunted me until I got started writing.

My journey has been a spiritual one as much as it has been a business venture. I could not possibly thank all of the men and women who have impacted me. One I have to mention, however, is Dr. Don Ralston, whom I was learning from when my life experience was at a crossroads. He remains an example to me. While I was finishing this manuscript, Dr. Willy Rice and Danny Bennett were likewise very helpful.

Like many young men, I was blessed to have teachers who did more than teach me; they powerfully affected my thinking and my decisions. I write about several of them in this book, but one in particular deserves a special thank-you. Dr. James "Chester" Gibson, retired dean of the University of West Georgia and one of the most esteemed coaches in the history of intercollegiate debate, taught me life lessons that I still follow decades later. Outside my family, no one has influenced my life for good more than Dr. Gibson has.

I have dedicated this book to my clients, and I am also grateful to all of them for inviting me to share in their work. One client especially, Gene McNichols, and his family—Scott, Steven, and Jennifer—have been unwavering in their support of my professional growth. I am indebted to them.

Finally, I want to thank the team at Greenleaf Book Group: Kris Pauls, Justin Branch, Alan Grimes, Sheila Parr, and all of the staff who have made this book a reality. Special thanks to Linda O'Doughda, who helped craft my experience into a clearer and more helpful story than I could ever have imagined.

There are so many more that I should mention. I hope, however, that I have already told you personally what you have meant to me. Life is a journey, and the people with whom we travel are our most valuable assets. They are also a gift. The best way we can acknowledge that is to become a gift in someone else's life. And that has been my goal in writing this book.

INTRODUCTION

. . . .

Recently I was sitting with a colleague of mine, and he asked me a very pointed question: "Barry, most advisors write their book early in their career and then build their business around it. Why did you wait so long?" It wasn't a hard question to answer. "Because I had to live what this book teaches before I could write about it," I said. "And I almost missed it!" I had set out to prove myself a leader, but I hadn't learned that the whole point of leading is having people who willingly follow you!

I got that sudden wake-up call from my associates, but I didn't even realize I was asleep! I wasn't quite twenty-seven years old and I found myself managing a nationwide company. Until that moment, I had been leaping up the ladder of success. Or so I thought. I had the title of "leader" but knew little about what it takes to earn the right to be followed. I had the wrong idea about what leadership was.

If I had ignored the warning of my associates, I could have missed ever learning how to become a lasting leader. Thankfully, I didn't ignore them. Starting that day, and during the decades thereafter, I discovered what you are going to read about in this book. Fortunately, you don't have to wait that long; you can learn from my experience now and begin to develop enthusiastic and engaged followers immediately.

In 30-plus years as a leader in both the public and the private sector, I have learned that leadership isn't just something you do, it's someone you become. This book is about what it takes to become the kind of person others will follow. It's about how to find the wisdom that can produce great results over and over again. And it's about the secret that lies in helping others discover their greatness. This is not a "how-to book," however. It's more of a "who are you becoming?" book. It's the book I wished I had read when I was just starting out as a manager and a leader of people.

You might be like a lot of leaders today. You're halfway through your career, and what has been working suddenly won't. You are trying to succeed by meeting your numbers like you always have, but it's more difficult to get your team to perform. The old motivational tricks are no longer enough to inspire loyalty. You are just entering your prime years, but the rules of leading have changed. You know you have to change, but you don't know how.

I know that feeling because I was once right there. You have been making progress but you feel something is missing. You can't quite seem to succeed for more than a few years at a time before you have to switch jobs or maybe even companies. Your back might even be against the wall right now, and you feel that time is running out for you to make a difference as a leader. Don't give up yet, and don't settle for being just an average manager. There is a better way if you are willing to discover it.

Leadership isn't just something you do; it's someone you become.

First, acknowledge that you are motivated to lead and that you have worked hard. Then, realize that hard work alone isn't enough anymore. Lasting leaders have to be able to take a diverse team and win quickly. Finally, embrace the principles you will learn from this book and do just that—win followers. The life lessons you will read about will show you how to finally become the kind of leader you have been striving to be. There is a leadership strategy with staying power that rescued my career, and I wrote this book to share it with you.

I am going to tell you about my own awakening and what I discovered. I'm also going to tell you about some of the leaders I have advised and coached over the years and how they stopped, took stock of themselves, and found a new way of leading that really works. And if you follow what this book teaches then, like them, you will find your success as a lasting leader too.

Remember, though, that success is not about more money or even more authority. It's really about influence: the influence that results in associates and employees wanting to follow your lead because of the person you have become. This is not just about my journey; it can become your journey as well.

You will quickly see that this is not just another business exercise. It's a lifelong process and experience. You will become not only a better leader but also a better partner, better parent, and better friend. I know because it happened to me. And I am confident that I can help you discover your gifts as a leader who earns the right to be followed.

CHAPTER 1

LEARNING TO LEAD— THE HARD WAY

. . . .

Sometimes it takes getting what you have always wanted to discover what you really need. I always wanted to be a manager. My earliest jobs as a kid convinced me that I wanted to be the one making the decisions and not just doing the work. And with one phone call to my house in Atlanta on a very bright June afternoon in 1975 it happened.

On the other end of the phone was the owner of a chain of radio stations who was calling me back after an interview I had had with him a few weeks earlier. I was only twenty-three years old, but I had been working in broadcasting since my early teens. I knew what it took to produce the kind of programming that would draw an audience. The owner offered me the job as general manager of his broadcasting company in Baltimore. I had barely hung up the phone when I began to dance around my living room. My dream had come true! I was being given what I thought I wanted and needed—the reins of leadership. But what I really needed was to know *how* to be a leader, and my painful lessons on leadership were about to begin.

I TRIED THE TRADITIONAL TOOLS.

Every new manager thinks he's ready to be a leader. I certainly did. I had my folders all labeled: 90-day plan, employee review forms, short-term goals, financial goals, company policies and procedures. I was ready. There was nothing wrong with those file folders I had prepared for my new role as the radio station's general manager. Planning, evaluations, and financial goals are important! But those items are not the most important topic a leader needs to consider in order to start out on the right foot. And that would be a folder labeled in all caps—PEOPLE!

Had I picked up on a mentor's hint she gave me before I left Atlanta, I might not have made the mistakes that I did in that first management role.

"You mean that YOU are going to be the GENERAL MANAGER of the station?" I had stopped by to tell my first boss in broadcasting my great news before I left for Baltimore. At the time, I thought she was just surprised and happy for me. But I realize now that she was really suggesting I wasn't up for the job. That even with all of my experience I was lacking something. Had I asked why she was shocked at my being named to the top spot, she would probably have politely told me what I needed to hear: "You're smart enough for the job, Barry, but if you want to *lead* people then you have a lot to learn *about* people."

And she would know. Grace and her husband Carol Lee hired me when I was fourteen. The Lees ran their small community station like stewards of a great community trust. They carried the only local news available to listeners in the area. Even though most of the local population would have preferred around-the-clock country music, Grace and Carol insisted on carrying a variety, from rock to easy listening and even some gospel now and again.

Music wasn't the only thing they broadcast. Each year there would be a "Rotary Day" when local Rotary Club members took turns as DJs for the day to raise money. The Lees were not just owners of this little radio station; they had become the heartbeat of the community.

I realized how valuable they were to our town, but somehow I didn't make the connection between the way they interacted with the townspeople and the way they led the two or three of us who worked for them. Each of us was more than an employee to them. They cared about my family and showed genuine interest in all the things I was involved in at the only high school in our county. I wish now that I had paid more attention to their example as leaders whose remarkable concern for others was more than just a strategy; it was who they were.

Two days after saying good-bye to everyone, I was on final approach to Baltimore/Washington International Airport. I still remember how proud I felt taking a plane to my new job. Most of my buddies back in Georgia traveled to work in their pickup truck. I gathered my luggage and went out to meet my new employee who had come to welcome me and give me a ride.

I've wished a thousand times to have that ride from the airport to take over again. I would have used the opportunity to get to know this fellow and open up to him. I would have made every effort to send the message that not only was I willing to listen but also that I needed to listen to him and the other employees if we were all to succeed together.

I really wasn't rude; I was just disinterested in him personally. I wanted to know about our competition. I wanted to know about our equipment and how well we were set up to expand. I wanted to know all the things that would be important to growing the station but had little to do with growing the team or my relationship with them.

It's been an ongoing fear of mine in subsequent decades that he would show up in a seminar I was leading or a conference where I was speaking on "lasting leadership." In my nightmare, he jumps up in the middle of my presentation and starts shouting "HYPOCRITE!" And just when I start to explain to him that I changed and became a different kind of person, I wake up—usually in a cold sweat!

Throughout our drive north past the city, I told him about my strategic plan and how I wanted to motivate the employees by using clear performance measures. I had ideas about how to improve our programming lineup and sell more airtime. Never once did I ask him a question about his job, his ideas, his aspirations. Thinking back on it, I recall that he didn't respond directly to me but his body language was saying, "Who does this guy think he is?"

He dropped me at my hotel, and I got ready for day 1 of my new life. The owner of the station was in town, and he had spent the prior few days dismissing the current general manager to make way for me—his new young protégé. He especially liked it that I could read the P&L statements and that I readily accepted his financial goals. For my part, I viewed authority as the key requirement to leading others, and he had given me the very title that would mean I had all the authority necessary.

It takes more than the ability to read a P&L statement or the authority embedded in a title to be a leader who can last for more than a few years, however. Nevertheless, I honestly thought that if my staff would just do what I said, we all would succeed financially as well as have wonderful careers— together. In other words, if you couldn't buy in to my plan and my way of running the business, then there must be something inherently wrong with you.

The staff didn't openly resist my ideas, but they did voice their own opinions, some of which were based on years in the market. For example, we carried a half-hour program on Sunday morning that was produced in the "Little Italy" section of Baltimore. It was a mixture of music and talk, but my problem with the show was that it was done entirely in Italian. This meant that I had to pay a translator to listen to the broadcast and verify that no FCC regulations had been violated.

Over the objection of my staff I made the decision that all programming had to be in English and this program was canceled. They tried to impress upon me that it had been on the air for more than twenty years and to convince me that the sponsor of the show was one of the leading Italian businessmen in town. I didn't listen.

I wish I had. Ten days after I took the program off the air we had a visitor in our lobby who identified himself as an attorney for the sponsor. The secretary brought him to my office, and before he could sit down I repeated my decision and reminded him that I was the new general manager of the station and had the authority to do what I had done.

Thirty minutes later, I began to get *his message*. This Italian sponsor wasn't going anywhere. If anybody was going somewhere it was going to be the station's "general manager," who had just arrived in town. I put the program back on the schedule immediately, and it remained on the air for decades!

Learning to listen to my employees and value their opinions was something I would have to learn the hard way. I wasn't growing the staff. In fact, I was alienating them. But my first year of financial success kept me from experiencing that problem as soon as I might have. It was only later that I realized this truth: if you are not building relationships that will last with your associates, your financial success will be short-lived.

I GREW THE BOTTOM LINE BUT SABOTAGED MY RELATIONSHIPS WITH MY TEAM AND DIDN'T EVEN REALIZE IT.

My first year in Baltimore was, as I said, a financial success but not so successful by any other measure. We had new programs and new advertisers. We expanded our reach into the community, and despite a tough economic environment, we grew the profit margin. But I pushed my employees (who were loyal and wanted to do what I asked) hard and required them to follow my direction, and I could change my mind quickly. As a result, the staff were constantly having to make last-minute adjustments. This uncertainty consumed resources and sapped their emotional energy. Regardless of my intentions, it was a poor way to build a cohesive team.

> If you're not building relationships that will last with your associates, your financial success will be short-lived.

My direction could often come on a whim. I would be out to lunch with a client, for example, and be asked if we could do a remote broadcast for them or help them with a community project. My answer was always YES. I didn't bother to ask my team if we could do it. I didn't get their input about how we would staff the event. I just overcommitted them and expected them to fix it.

Because I was making such commitments of time and resources, my employees were constantly scrambling. If they gave me any resistance I wouldn't hesitate to start looking at applications from prospective new employees. Eventually I drove them to do things we couldn't do or, worse yet, forgot that I had committed us to something in the first place.

Obviously (but not to me then), as a result of this approach, I was not building loyalty. And I was not creating an atmosphere of excellence. To the contrary, I was developing a team that was hesitant to act independently with confidence, because they couldn't trust me to communicate the direction we were going. In other words, if you worked for me you were better off just waiting for me to tell you exactly what to do. Thinking on your own was probably not going to be rewarded.

This would have been the perfect time to slow down and face my dilemma, to learn how to build mutually respectful and ultimately profitable relationships with my employees. But I didn't see it as a problem. As long as the numbers added up at the end of the month, we must be on the right track.

At the pace I was going there was bound to be a lot of turnover. Yet I didn't know how to build a team or even how to identify the best players. From my perspective, money was always the biggest motivator; with the right amount of it, you could get anyone to do whatever you asked. I didn't understand how important it was to build a relationship with your employees first before you expected them to do your bidding.

It was about this time my owner offered me the position of executive vice president and general manager of not only our Baltimore operation but also his Cincinnati station and our new acquisitions in Toledo and shortly thereafter Los Angeles and Tampa. In just two years since receiving that life-changing phone call in Atlanta, I was responsible for all of the stations in our network!

Have you ever gotten a promotion or maybe a job offer just in the "nick of time"? My sudden promotion removed any possibility that I would take a candid look in the mirror and start behaving like a leader and not just a business-savvy manager. I set my sights on the horizon. There were new stations to open and new goals to meet. After all, I had been promoted for a reason.

Promotions don't cure leadership flaws.

Those in-the-nick-of-time promotions just cover up our weaknesses. The house was making money, but it was a house of cards. I now know that I should have invested more time in my employees. But rather than take a deep breath and reflect on how I was beginning to fail in my previous assignment, I—like many other businesspeople do—took the new opportunity as proof that I was really as good as I thought I was!

But what if we are not as good as we think we are? What if our employees are only telling us what they think we want to hear? If that's the case, then we will miss the critical information we need to make good decisions.

Remember the debacle Toyota had with their "accidental acceleration" problem? As it turns out, the top management had been shielded from negative data. Consequently, they repeatedly denied there was an accelerator issue. That delay before they finally admitted the obvious was costly. That data would have helped them avert a disaster.

If managers are to succeed at leading, they have to work with teams that can speak candidly with them, without fear that the leader will lose his or her self-confidence, self-control, or self-esteem. Any communication short of that will not be enough. I was lucky to receive that kind of candid talk—from the most unlikely place. Despite the fact that I hadn't encouraged it and, quite frankly, hadn't asked for it.

With my promotion came relocation to our largest station, a 50,000-watt powerhouse in Tampa. This would mean a lot of travel to each market, from Baltimore to Los Angeles. But my energy was concentrated in Tampa at our newest acquisition and soon-to-be flagship property. This was in the days before email, so our messages from other associates came in the mail.

The front office secretary would go through everything and then distribute it. One day she dropped a letter on my desk and headed back up front. She had no idea that that particular letter would be the catalyst for my awakening. Neither did I.

Promotions don't cure leadership flaws.

Glancing at the return address on the envelope, I saw that the letter was from our Baltimore station. And as I unfolded it, I recognized the names listed at the bottom. What kind of letter would those guys write together and send to me? As I read the first lines, I saw that they got to the point quickly. They politely told me they had no interest in working with me in the future! They believed that it was only a matter of time until I failed big-time as a leader because of the way I had interacted with them, other staff, and even customers.

Specifically, they said I had failed them as their leader on several counts: *You don't listen to us. You make promises to us and then don't deliver on them. You change priorities so often we can't trust your decisions. You don't value us! You see us as means to an end . . .* and so on. Pretty tough words from people you thought were your friends. With the benefit of time, I now recognize they were, indeed, acting like true friends by confronting me.

If the letter had been mean-spirited I would have just dismissed it out of hand. But this was different. These men were all Christians who gave more than lip service to their faith. And that's the attitude they conveyed in the words of that letter. They showed appreciation for what I had accomplished but thought the way I had done it was unacceptable.

It really doesn't matter how any of us comes to realize that we need to work on our leadership skills. The point each of us must ask is, what am I going to do about it? A lot of leaders simply blame their followers and move on. Others blame their circumstances and just live to repeat the same behavior.

But there are a few, and I am blessed to be among them, who neither blame their circumstances nor continue to repeat the same behavior for a lifetime.

Instead, they get serious about examining what it takes to lead effectively and repeatedly over a long period of time. But I didn't do that right away.

At first I replayed in my head all of my actions during the previous two years, and I could counter each of their criticisms with a corresponding management strategy that proved successful. But that was shallow. These men weren't disputing my ability to produce results; they were distancing themselves from me because they didn't want to work in the kind of environment I had fostered.

And, after thinking about the content of their letter for several weeks, I realized I didn't want to work in that kind of environment either. If you produce results but lose the support of your team then you will forever be building a new team. Hardly a formula for genuine success.

There was enough truth in what they said, and enough of my original goal to be an effective leader still in me, that I decided to try to change. But substituting one set of motivational gimmicks for another would be a lateral move. I would have to think hard about what real change in my leadership would look like.

I had begun teaching a night class at a local private Christian college in addition to my day job among the broadcast group. The subject was "communication," so it was a perfect fit for me to do more research on what separates lasting leaders from those who can stay in the game for only a season.

Have you had trouble lasting for more than a season? Is that why you are reading this book? Like me, have you gotten just enough feedback to realize that you can't reach the next level in your company, your community, or your life if you don't make the transition from one who acts like a leader to one who lives like a leader? Perhaps knowing what I did at my own crossroads will help you make your next move.

I MADE A DECISION TO RESIGN.

My boss agreed to meet with me at the Tampa Airport. We took a booth in the hotel restaurant near the terminal. It was a quick conversation.

I explained to him that I wanted to step aside and work full-time at the college where I was teaching so I could learn alongside the students about how to lead *with purpose and passion*. The college needed my help and I knew it would be a chance for me to grow. He thought I was fine as a manager and didn't see a problem. But I felt that I was not a competent leader. Although I was very good at making change happen, to lead at the most successful level would take more than just knowing the numbers.

The company owner wasn't impressed with my decision. And as he began to explain what it would cost me financially to walk away from my employment agreement, I will admit that I had second thoughts. But the words from that letter still haunted my mind, and I knew what I had to do. I had come to realize that a leader's true power comes from influence, not authority.

You can't fake influence. In Texas they have the disparaging remark, "He's all hat, no cattle." In other words, he's acting like something he's not. If I knew anything after resigning from the radio stations I managed it was this: I would not fake it anymore!

My decision to resign was less than a day old when the aging president of the college, a man of great faith and vision, asked me to join his team to help him in the transition to a new president, who would not be able to serve full-time. Since it was a private Christian college my compensation would be minimal, but the opportunity to grow would prove to be invaluable. He had asked me before but now was the right time, the right move for my awakening. I would be in a supportive learning environment while taking the best of what I knew and sharing it with students not that much younger than me. It was a quick exit strategy with a soft landing.

It was more difficult to take that job than I thought it would be, however. I was immediately cast into a leadership role that stirred my "old" expedient leadership style because I had not yet fully grasped what the "right" leadership style was. But I was more open and ready to learn a replacement style.

And I was able to help the school make significant advancements in their physical plant, their accreditation, and their approach to students.

In fact, within a few years I was asked to move from being in the administration of the new president to becoming the president of the college. At that point the school needed someone who could get results in fundraising, student development, and greater community awareness. And although I was focused on understanding how lasting leaders make the transition to living like a leader, there was still a lot of "let's go reach the goal" in me. That's exactly what the college needed.

Little by little I was inching forward. When some of the weeds of my former management style popped up, I would mow them down—only to see new ones sprout. I had planned to be at the college for just a few short years, but the tasks to accomplish were daunting, and we were making progress. So I stayed for more than a decade, which was a year or two longer than I should have.

Luckily when my years as an administrator and professor came to an end, three specific events put the final shape to my growth as a leader. First, the governor of Florida, who had observed my work in turning the college around, asked me to serve in his administration as a member of the State Board of Independent Colleges and Universities. Second, I continued to volunteer by teaching a community Bible class. Third, I joined the leadership team of a highly successful training company in Tampa.

As the governor's appointee, I had to work with people both within his political party and across the aisle. Real negotiation on issues affecting the lives of hundreds of thousands of college students required the leaders involved to be collaborative.

This was my do-over. Instead of trying to be the smartest person in the room, I began to build professional relationships based on mutually beneficial goals. That meant *really* getting to know every member of the team. I vividly remember one afternoon when I was meeting with our state board staff and asked them their opinion about a pending matter. I didn't interrupt them, and I didn't even spout off my own idea. Rather, I caught myself listening. I was no longer in the small world of the radio stations or the friendly halls of academia. But I was also not the same leader I had been.

While I was still at the college, I had read constantly about the lives of leaders who had lasted. Searching for clues in each person was my constant vigil. And slowly but subtly I began to notice that their followers often responded similarly to their leadership. They would make comments like, "I always felt like he listened to me." Or "I was more than just an employee. He really cared about me." Or "He was quick to recognize when I had done a good job."

I tried to build those values into my life as I went on to serve governors Bob Martinez, Lawton Chiles, and Jeb Bush. One was not from my political party and I tried to resign upon his election, only to be asked by the local leader of his party to stay on for another term because, as he put it, I knew "how to get diverse people to take common action."

My fellow board members likewise recognized my work and elected me to back-to-back terms as chairman of the State Board of Independent Colleges and Universities. We had regulatory oversight of a 100-plus colleges and universities, with better than half a million students, and our leadership was scrutinized constantly by our constituents, the legislature, and the press.

I not only survived that scrutiny; I thrived through it. Leadership that begins by putting others' interests first has the strength to forge lasting relationships. For the first time in my business career, I saw that reality coming to life in and for me as a leader.

While I was leading state board initiatives across the state I was also teaching a Bible class to businesspeople and other individuals who were seeking to better understand life and faith. This forced me to study ancient truths about how ethical relationships are formed in humility, compassion, and even love. Our group would study on Monday night, and I would try to apply what we learned throughout the rest of the week.

Sometimes it would be three steps forward and two steps back, but the momentum was steady. The words of the letter that challenged my very right to lead kept motivating me to find a better way to lead. They also motivated me to become a better person. I wasn't focused any longer on just "techniques" or "tactics." I began to see leadership as an expression of who I was and not just what I did in my career.

Bring out the best in others.

Serving others as their leader is not about lip service or a title on a door. It's a way of life. A transparent and giving life that is dedicated to bringing out the best in others—especially those who look to you as their leader.

A giving life inspires followers to embrace both you and your goals. Perhaps no one has evidenced that more than Frances Hesselbein. Between 1965 and 1976 she went from being a volunteer Girl Scout leader to becoming the nonprofit's CEO—the first to come from within the ranks in 67 years. She held that job for more than fourteen years, during which time she is widely credited with turning the organization around while growing membership to 2.25 million and a workforce in excess of 700,000.

Years ago Peter Drucker, the father of modern management, was asked who he thought was the greatest leader in America. Since he had consulted with the likes of Jack Welch and most of the Fortune 100 leaders, his answer came as a surprise. Without hesitancy Drucker replied, "Francis Hesselbein, the CEO of the American Girl Scout movement. She could manage any company in America."[1]

And now the real question, how did she do it? Hesselbein has been quoted repeatedly saying that one of her secrets is, "The first item in your budget should be learning, education, and development of your people."[2] And she developed the now legendary approach of "circular management," where the leader sat in the middle of the organization chart, not at the top. From that perspective, the leader can better plan, guide, and inspire performance. Our current economic realities now require that kind of leadership.

> Leadership that begins by putting
> others' interests first has the strength
> to forge lasting relationships.

My work life was correspondingly supporting my personal growth. Scott and Terry Hitchcock, who owned a prosperous training franchise in Tampa, helped me immensely to become a better person. They actually reminded me of Grace and Carol Lee, who had hired me as a teenager to work for their rural radio station. Scott and Terry put me in a leadership position over their sales team while at the same time allowing me to learn timeless principles about the very kind of leader I wanted to become by teaching leadership training classes.

What I was learning as I prepared to lead training sessions could be applied in my public role as well. All of this growth could have occurred back in Baltimore, but it didn't because of one significant fact: at that time I didn't see the need to grow as a leader; my focus was solely on the bottom line.

I started out as a manager thinking my job was to sit at the top, but over time I began to move toward the middle, where I could lead with influence. These experiences continued to shape me. What's shaping your growth as a leader right now? Are you leading from the middle, or are you stuck trying to command from the top? Which are you relying on, authority or influence?

With the advantage of years I can look back and see just how important those self-focused years in broadcasting and the self-sacrificing years in private education were in my development. Both served me well to prune and strengthen me. And during those years I began to see what it was about some leaders that made them last. They had in common an approach to working with people that earned them the right to be followed. That's not just another strategy, however; it's more of a lifelong journey. I hope the experience of reading this book and going online (www.aleadersgift.com) and taking the leader's gift assessments will inspire you to become a fellow traveler!

CHAPTER 2

THE WAY OUT IS IN!

. . . .

It's not a new debate. Are leaders made or are they born? You've probably heard during such discussions expressions like "She's just got a gift for it" or "He's a natural." There's no denying that our DNA does impact a lot of our traits and characteristics, and some of those are more conducive to our becoming a leader.

But I maintain that every single one of us has the seeds of great leadership within us. Only a few will do the work to discover them, however, and even fewer will invest the time and effort necessary to reap a harvest of influence.

What are these traits that successful leaders are made of? Where do you find them? How do you begin to develop them in a way that will work for you?

If we want to understand what really defines leaders, I suggest that we start by looking at their followers. What causes some people to willingly follow one person while strongly resisting the lead of someone else? Is it really just a matter of preference?

Look to your own life. Ask yourself what drew you to certain people and turned you away from others. What was it about some people that made them exceptional leaders? It was when I started asking these questions of myself that I began to see patterns emerging that work—and they make sense.

> If we want to understand what really
> defines leaders, I suggest we start
> by looking at their followers.

Two men in particular demonstrated for me the traits of a leader who draws people to him by being open to others and encouraging them. My experience with each man was decades apart, but their approach to leading was the same.

Beecher Duvall grew up in Atlanta in a family that afforded him the best education and a lot of incentive to finish college and launch his career in the city. But he had other plans.

Beecher chose to locate a couple of hours north of Atlanta in a rural mountain community. And that's when I met him. He was our high school guidance counselor and my scout leader. We were used to people from Atlanta coming up to the mountains for the summer to cool off, and they usually were a bit "cool" toward us native mountain people as well.

But Beecher wasn't that way. From the very beginning he opened up to us and our way of life and gave us a chance. I have no memory of him—whether as teacher or scoutmaster—being anything but ready to listen to and encourage me. He was always looking for a way to help us grow.

One spring he called me into his office and told me about a program being offered for a term at Phillips Andover Academy just north of Boston. He said they might even give special consideration to applicants from more deprived parts of the country.

Beecher urged me to apply. I remember taking the literature home and thinking that there was no way someone like me from the foothills of Appalachia could do this. Even my parents thought the notion was farfetched. After all, Andover is one of the most acclaimed prep schools in American history. Among the eminent alumni are a number of presidents, governors, and senators. Yet if I applied and was accepted, it could be the most pivotal experience of my education and maybe even my life.

My family would have never dreamed of trying to achieve that kind of opportunity, but Beecher dreamed it for us, and it came true. That summer I kissed my mother good-bye, shook my dad's hand, and boarded a bus bound for Boston. Indeed it was the single most important educational experience of my life, thanks to a leader who saw something in me I couldn't see.

When leaders take the risk to place their confidence in us, even before we have earned it, it gives us the strength to face adversity without excuse. It gives us the courage to live beyond our self-imposed limits!

How about you? Was your earliest memory of a genuine leader a teacher? A coach? An advisor? Take a moment to think back on your relationship. What is it now, as an adult, that you appreciate about how that person influenced you? I bet you won't have to look hard to find some of the same behaviors in your early influencers that I did. And you will see the connection between those leaders' behaviors and your own achievements.

The second leader who drew me in by how he listened to and encouraged me is successful businessman and philanthropist Joe White. He became a client after I began my consulting practice and then a valued friend.

Joe came home from the Vietnam War expecting to join his father's business, Castle Supply. But when, while touring the company's Sarasota, Florida, branch, Joe's dad announced that Joe was the new branch manager, left him there, and wished him luck, Joe was flabbergasted. In his twenties, newly married, and just home from the army, this definitely wasn't what he expected.

I don't think Joe understands to this day why he didn't run, but he didn't! He stuck it out and learned the business on the fly—one customer at a time. Joe faced the normal tension of every young business leader: do I pay attention to customers first or employees? But Joe didn't give in to the temptation to choose one over the other. He decided to invest in both. And by leading like this for more than three decades, he grew this small family business into a national leader in their industry.

Since he sold his company (see the box titled "Lasting leaders end well.") I have worked with Joe in several endeavors where he has been a volunteer leader with a significant responsibility. And I have watched him help some of his protégés start a new business. Joe treats them all just like he treated his family's enterprise: he puts the people first!

Joe could go into any business, for profit or not, and lead it to thrive because

Lasting leaders end well.

I actually met Joe White through one of those men he chose to invest in—Bob Cardwell. Bob began working for Joe at the entry level. He grew to the role of a branch manager and by the time we met he was the president of Castle Supply, with Joe as CEO. As I looked around this very profitable company with multiple locations, I saw a pattern. There were men and women in every branch and most departments who had a story to tell about how Joe White had taken a chance on them and then stood back and let them grow. In return Joe had a team of loyal employees who put customers first—every time.

I began to work with Joe and Bob, helping develop their leadership team and document strategic planning for his company, which kept growing year after year. In fact, that unprecedented growth created what most people would see as a windfall but actually was a dilemma for Joe. An international company that also was a major force in the same industry across the U.S. put an offer on the table to buy his company that Joe couldn't ignore. But the family's first concern was the people who worked for them.

They worried about their employees. How would those associates be impacted by a sale? How would the new owner treat them? I hurried to his office when I got the call that he wanted to talk to me immediately. I shut the door behind me and sat down uncertain about what I was about to hear.

But what I heard didn't surprise me. What I heard from Joe White was first, his concern about how his family would react to selling the business, and second, what this would do to his employees. The advice he was looking to me for was how to protect both. He never mentioned himself.

Over the next several months Joe would negotiate the sale of his company. And at every step he was calculating how to keep his family's interest foremost and how could he protect his employees. In fact, during one meeting in his office a competitor, another national company with a brand name known in every household, called and made Joe an offer. Whatever amount the buyer had agreed to the caller was willing to beat. Joe never gave it a thought because he knew this suitor would not be fair with his associates and he wasn't willing to compromise that for any amount!

The closing day came and those long-term employees, including the president, Bob Cardwell, were rewarded for their loyalty. In fact, I have never seen any other business owner leave as much on the table for his associates. He also took part of the sale and formed The White Family Foundation so his wife and daughters could continue supporting those issues that mattered to them.

he believes that people build businesses and organizations. It's his job to find the best people and lead them by giving himself to them until they can fly on their own. And that's why people are drawn to him. I once asked Joe why he worked so hard and he quickly replied, "For me it's all about my family." At that moment I realized that his definition of family included not only the ones who bear his name but also everyone who comes under his influence.

Like Beecher Duvall, Joe White was open, he listened without judging, he invested time in me, he encouraged me continuously, and he appreciated my strengths. And because of that I followed his lead.

Putting others first is the secret to successful leadership. The leader who is focused on himself starts with his plan and his goal. But the leader who is focused on others starts with her team. What do they need to succeed? How can the leader equip them to win? What's important to them?

Take a look at your own team. What kind of turnover have you had? How many "A" players do you have? Is your team nimble enough to change directions quickly and willingly? The answers to these questions are like a leadership CT scan and will be valid predictors of your success as a leader.

FOLLOWERS WILL BE DRAWN TO YOUR OPENNESS, INVESTMENT OF TIME, LISTENING, ENCOURAGEMENT, AND APPRECIATION.

I have studied hundreds of leaders and have researched hundreds more. A few months after I opened my management consulting practice (and while I was earning my certification from the Institute of Management Consultants), I was writing a leadership development program for a Fortune 100 company. Suddenly, the pieces of the lasting leadership puzzle fell into place.

I had been asking myself for years: what were the traits that lasting leaders had in common? What were the things I was missing as a young leader that led to my failure as a manager? And what had I observed that seemed to motivate employees to extraordinary performance?

In a moment I realized that great leaders don't focus on *getting*. They're all about *giving* something away, freely and frequently. They give something away that money can't buy and that the receiver wouldn't sell for any price. They give the gift of themselves.

These 5 qualities are gifts because it's only when we give them away freely to everyone in our path that they create in us the life qualities of a lasting leader. The 5 qualities you'll learn to give away are

The Gift of Being Open to other people.

The Gift of Investing Time in other people.

The Gift of Listening to other people.

The Gift of Offering Encouragement to other people.

The Gift of Expressing Appreciation for other people.

These gifts appear to be simple, perhaps even obvious. Anything truly inspirational always does. But it is their simplicity that requires more than

Beware the numbers leadership trap.

When I took my first business leader's role as a broadcasting GM, it wasn't that I was completely wrong. I wasn't. But I was only *half right*. Of course you have to focus on the numbers, whether you're responsible for the monthly bottom line or the production goals. Everything gets measured and you will ultimately be evaluated on the numbers.

But that's a leadership trap. It is so tempting just to keep your eye on the scoreboard and make your moves with an eye toward winning. Over time, however, this approach will result in exhausting the people you lead. And while you are running up the score, you are running down the very people who got you there.

Randy Gage, a leading writer and coach on personal performance, puts it this way: "If you are asking the wrong question, then the answer is irrelevant!"[1] If your only question is how much did we make, how many did we produce, and how many did we ship, then your answer will not be relevant to your lasting success.

That's why the usual management question of how to get more out of people for less is foolish. You may get short-term results, but eventually you will burn those people out and the cost of recruiting, hiring, and training new personnel will eat away at whatever profit you thought you were producing.

Be careful, though; it's also true that in focusing only on people you could limit profit. And remember that many good things follow profit: Profit allows pay raises, retirement contributions, investments in growth, and even charitable gifts. Profit is a noble goal! It just can't be the only goal.

Because if you don't focus on the people who produce the profit you will be on a constant rollercoaster of quick growth and painful setbacks. Put people first and then you will know how to deploy the right people with the right skills at just the right time to create loyal and repeat customers!

When you are balancing profit with people, you are also better equipped to know which people should stay on your team. Here is a little-known secret about what happens when you learn how to understand the people you lead. You recognize much sooner those people who shouldn't be on your team. It doesn't mean they are bad people; it simply means that they are not the right fit for your team.

Balance people along with a collaborative approach to leading and you will produce the results you are looking for. Get unbalanced on either the profit or the people side and you will be forever chasing the wind as a leader. It's like standing in a rowboat and abruptly shifting your weight from one side to the other. The boat rocks. Everything in the boat is tossed about. You start creating waves. And before long you are out of the boat!

just a passing nod from us. It's not enough to applaud them. To become a lasting leader means you have to embrace them while still focusing on the metrics that define your progress. The two are linked together. (See the box titled "Beware the numbers leadership trap" in this chapter.) You can't choose which one to follow because without both of them your leadership experience will be just another story of "what might have been."

These qualities aren't things you have; rather, they are things you give away. They require you to become someone who can give freely, without reservation, to the people you lead. Lasting leaders, by definition, devote their energy toward the people they lead—*first*. (When you put others first, you won't become second. On the contrary, you will become more valuable to your team, your company, than any authority could ever mandate!)

Leaders who are held in the highest esteem for their success on both the bottom line and with the people they lead epitomize these five qualities. And the really great news is that it's never too late to embrace them as gifts. Not gifts you possess but, rather, gifts you will freely give to others. You can recognize these lasting leaders by the way their followers describe them. You will hear phrases like these: "He was always there for me," "I felt like she really listened," "He valued my opinion," and so forth. Let's have a look at each of these five qualities in a little more detail.

The Gift of Being Open to Others.

What would it be like to work for someone who was open to who you are? Not who they want you to be or the role they want you to play but the real you. What if you sensed that it mattered to them where you came from, what motivated you, and what your innermost hopes and dreams were? And what if you believed that they could be trusted with those truths about you and would only use them to bring out the best in you and align you with their goals for joint success?

You would consider that a gift and you would consider yourself blessed! You would place much higher value on that relationship and be more prone to preserve it through your improved performance. That's the gift of *openness*.

The Gift of Investing Time in Others.

What would it be like to have a boss who had time for you? Not just when they wanted something, but as a matter of routine they dropped by your workspace? And what if they didn't have any certain agenda; they just thought it would be valuable to spend more of their time with you?

I am necessarily not talking about out-of-the-office time. I am thinking of a boss who chooses to invest time in you as a priority in his or her workday.

How would that affect the way you valued your role at work? You couldn't help but feel as though you were important to them, right? And there is the high likelihood that over time you would return this gift by showing a return on the leader's investment of time in you.

We all have differing amounts of money and wealth. But we all possess exactly the same amount of time each day. When a leader chooses to spend moments with you, that's the gift of *time invested in you*.

The Gift of Listening to Others.

What would it be like to work for someone who listened to you? I am not talking about whether or not they heard your words. I mean they genuinely listened. Listeners send the clear message that your thoughts are valuable and what you think is important to them.

How would it feel to have a boss who solicited your opinion while suspending judgment as to whether you were right or wrong? If you were able to have a candid conversation and were confident your thoughts would be given consideration before a decision was made, how would that impact your self-perception at work?

When we believe someone is really paying attention to us and hearing what we say, we automatically give that person credibility as a leader and are much more prone to listen the same way in return when they are speaking. It's painfully obvious that most people don't listen like this, and we've come not to expect it. When a leader does so we realize it is truly a gift. It's the gift of *listening*.

The Gift of Offering Encouragement to Others.

What would it be like to work for a leader who knew of your weaknesses and your daily challenges? Would it affect you positively for that same leader to encourage you that you can break through your barriers? What if that leader was able to articulate where you are in your performance and where you need to get to—all the while expressing total confidence that you were going to be able to do it? Would it make a difference if you felt that the leader would be there to cheer you on or help remove unforeseen obstacles?

Most of us work for someone who is more adept at catching us doing something wrong and pointing it out! Having a leader who encouraged us unconditionally would be a once-in-a-lifetime experience, a gift. The gift of *encouragement.*

The Gift of Expressing Appreciation for Others.

Would it make any difference to you if you worked for someone who was constantly pointing out what you had done well to contribute to your company's success? What if that person frequently praised you in public for your individual effort that was positively impacting the entire team? How would it feel to work for someone whose communication with you routinely included "Thank you very much"?

Most of us go through our adult lives with no one paying enough attention to us to even recognize when we do something well. We typically only hear from people when we have messed something up and it's impacting them. Working for someone who was constantly trying to catch us doing something right would be the gift of *appreciation.*

LASTING LEADERSHIP IS ALL ABOUT OTHERS—FIRST.

Have you ever given someone a gift that you couldn't wait for her to open? You had thought very carefully about what to give her. And you were pretty positive she was going to really love this gift. In fact, you were convinced she would treasure the gift for a long time. That is exactly the kind of observation, preparation, and giving of yourself that is required of a lasting leader.

The origin of these gifts is rooted in teachings from every ancient religion. Eternal truths like "do unto others," "put others' interests on par with your own," "pride will bring destruction," and "what a person thinks determines what he or she will do" are almost commonplace. They were not foreign to me; I had simply never thought of their application at work. In fact, I was more of the school that teaches that you don't have to develop these relationships at work. The way you live your personal life has nothing to do with your work life.

Most people, like I did, fail to embrace the five qualities because they require effort, sacrifice, and discipline. We would much rather have a "quick-fix trick" with which to wring out the last bit of productivity from the people who report to us.

But once you embrace them, and thus transition from who you are now to someone who is living and giving these qualities away, people will follow you with enthusiasm and loyalty. Not everyone, but far more followers than you ever dreamed possible.

Think back over your career. Did you ever have a leader who seemed to take extra time for you? Maybe he invested time before or after work to show you a better way to do something. Or maybe he welcomed your venting about challenges you were facing. Regardless of the situation, chances are you have often said of that leader things like, "He was really there for me," or "She was willing to take the time to teach me," or "He never made me feel like I was intruding."

Do you see now that the way admired leaders interacted with you was a gift? They weren't obligated to do it. There wasn't an immediate payoff for them. In fact, you might say, "It was just the way they were with everyone."

Chances are very good that those are the people who have influenced you the most in your professional development and maybe even personally. They didn't treat you with favoritism or preference. They just showed you an uncommon respect for being human!

The most successful leadership begins inside of you. It takes thought, planning, discipline, and often self-sacrifice. That's why quick management tricks don't work. Manipulation is about getting something quickly at the lowest possible price. A leader's gift that transforms his or her person, followers, and organization is about doing something over a lifetime at great personal cost of both time and vulnerability.

You may never have a boss who relates to you the way I just described. But here is wonderful news: *you* can become that kind of leader! And the people who report to you can say without hesitation that you are a gift to them. You don't need permission from anyone to become this kind of leader. It will not require a requisition form or a purchase order. All that's needed is for you to be willing to say, "I am ready to do the work to become the kind of person others will willingly follow until our success is guaranteed!"

So what do you think? Are lasting leaders made or are they just born that way? You might be able to find someone who won the genetic lottery and was born to lead and lead well. But that is not the case with you and me. If we are to become the leaders who succeed and make a difference while doing it, we have to become the kind of people whose first inclination is not to ask, what's in this for me? Instead we have to become the kind of people who instinctively wonder, who are the people working for me? What matters to them? How can I really listen to what they are saying? How can I make sure that I am investing enough time with them and building our relationship? How can I encourage them so they don't give up too soon? And what could I say to them that would help them value themselves and the contributions they are making to our effort?

It took me more than a decade to discover these truths and to struggle through my own transformation. Since then, my priority has been helping others see this much quicker and to achieve their personal growth much sooner and with far less difficulty. You can learn how to cultivate these five qualities and give them away. I am ready to show you how, and you have only to turn the page.

CHAPTER 3

THE GIFT OF BEING OPEN TO OTHERS

"I want to know *you!*"

. . . .

Every leader claims to have an open-door policy. In fact, so many executives repeat, "My door is always open," that it's the modern-day equivalent of the creditor dodge "the check is in the mail." It's an empty promise. And what's worse, an open-door policy without an open mind always leads to lost opportunity.

How many times a day do your employees knock on your office door and say, "I have an idea; do you have a minute?" If it is not happening at least once a day then there is a pretty good chance your employees would tell me that you are perpetually busy and don't have time for them.

Why don't you? I think it's really more a matter of personal preference than time. There are certain kinds of people we just don't relate to naturally. And when that kind of person happens to be working for us chances are we will convey—through our facial expressions, body language, and tone of voice—the notion that we are not interested in engaging with them.

> An open-door policy without an open
> mind always leads to lost opportunity.

But when we avoid the people who trouble us, we miss the opportunity to discover how to be more open with everyone. "Everything that irritates us about others can lead us to an understanding of ourselves" was how the legendary psychologist Carl Jung saw this dilemma.[1]

FIND THE GIFT
it's inside you!

Lasting leaders find the gift of openness by first looking inside themselves and admitting that they tend to discriminate against certain people. Then they make a commitment to not make that mistake again. Be honest with yourself. Give everyone who reports to you an opportunity to be heard, to be understood, and to be a part of what you are trying to accomplish.

Being open to others means being careful not to make assumptions. Instead, take the time to find out about them by asking questions such as these:

Who are they?

Where did they come from?

What has shaped their life and how they approach work?

What skills are they good at?

What unique knowledge do they possess?

What motivates them?

What's important to them right now?

How do they make decisions?

What are they afraid of?

What's their hidden dream?

What matters most to them?

Those are just the introductory questions that lasting leaders want to answer long before they start making assumptions about how to manage an employee. Do you know the answers to those questions about your current employees? Half of them? If not, then you are not open and you are not earning the right to be followed.

Be forewarned. This lack of openness and empathy for your team will potentially result in the inevitable slight on your part. You may not *intentionally* overlook or fail to hear someone on your team, but the impact is the same. And should this be your repeated behavior, you will develop a reputation for being less than courteous; more than likely, your associates might even in private describe you as rude.

Don't see that as a problem? Think again. *Harvard Business Review* recently polled 800 managers and employees across 17 industries. The workers who felt they had been treated with disrespect revealed the following;

48% intentionally decreased their work effort.

47% intentionally decreased the time spent at work.

38% intentionally decreased the quality of their work.

63% lost work time trying to avoid the offender.

66% said that their performance declined.

78% said that their commitment to the organization declined.

25% admitted to taking their frustrations out on customers.

Even if you cut these numbers in half, the tangible costs are staggering. Who can afford to have a workforce this disengaged because of the lack of civility in their working environment? The *Harvard Business Review* report prescribed an antidote: "Leaders can counter rudeness at work both by monitoring their own actions and by fostering civility in others."[2]

Everyone watches the leader. If he is open and hesitant to judge, then followers will mimic that, and when the leader monitors his own behavior, he will encourage others to do the same. One of the clearest examples I have seen of this came from a leader who had been at the helm of his family business in Connecticut for almost 50 years.

Everyone in the managers' meeting of the Plimpton and Hills Corporation near Hartford, Connecticut, was voicing their opinion. Tripp Hills, the president of the company, had encouraged them to do so. Some of the managers had decades of experience, and others were still new to leadership. Some had yet to prove themselves, while others were trying to recover from recent poor performance. One manager had even recently returned after having left to work for a competitor.

The decisions they were wrestling with had big-dollar impacts. Feelings were expressed passionately. But no one was cut off they spoke their mind. Sitting in the back of the room and taking it all in was the chairman of the board, seventy-two-year-old, Calvin Hills.

It takes personal humility to choose openness, and that's exactly what Calvin has done. His family business was founded in 1902. Calvin led the company for almost five decades, and the result was unprecedented success. He had every reason and every right to say, "I was leading this company before any of you were working . . . I will make these decisions on my own!"

But instead, Calvin listened to the management team and asked questions. He showed a genuine interest in their ideas, even the ones he had heard many times before. He practices openness with his managers for one reason: it pays big dividends. Calvin believes that when you show openness to all the ideas of your associates you will get their best, and their best will make you money!

Openness encourages employee engagement, and that is fundamental to business success. The *Ivey Business Journal* reported on the Gallup Organization's study of employee engagement in 7,939 business units in 36 different companies. It found that "employee engagement was positively associated with performance . . . About 2/3 of the business units scoring above the median on employee engagement also scored above the media on performance."[3]

Similarly, Thomas Petzinger researched businesses in forty cities and thirty states. In explaining the value of employee involvement in one company, Petzinger concluded: "[It] bred a culture of interaction in every corner of the plant. It reveals the creative power of human interaction."[4]

Few companies have practiced this kind of openness more than Southwest Airlines. Its founder and former CEO, Herb Kelleher, described the kind of leader this environment requires. "I have always believed that the best leader is the best servant."[5]

Recently Kelleher underscored the task of creating openness with employees when he told *Fortune* magazine: "If you're going to pay personal attention to each of your people, for instance, and every grief and every joy that they suffer in their lives, you really have to have a tremendous network for gathering information . . . It's not formulaic . . . It's something you do every day."[6]

Openness encourages employee engagement, and that is fundamental to business success.

It's not your door that needs to be open. It's your heart and your mind! Open those up to the people you lead and you will become the kind of leader who builds a winning team, and that team will build a winning business!

BUY INTO THE GIFT
it's a matter of choice!

Leaders who aren't open have a lot of excuses for why they can't behave this way. But the reasons they give ring hollow:

"My associates just want to know what to do."

"Being open would border on being too friendly."

"I would be viewed as too soft a leader if I did this."

Each of those statements tells me more about the leader than it does the followers. When you think you are the sole answer as to what to do, you have placed yourself in an impossible bind. You will be a bottleneck to your team's performance because they must constantly wait on you!

If you fear becoming friends with your associates, ask yourself exactly what you are afraid of. The answer I most often get is, "If I am their friend then I can't discipline them." Think this through. It means you are building your entire management philosophy on being free to discipline your employees. Think again. It is possible to be friendly with and open to another person without becoming their best friend forever or forfeiting the right to offer constructive comments. In fact, when you have demonstrated that you have employees' best interest at heart by how you have related to them, they are much more open to receiving your coaching. (See the box titled "Greater openness results in greater candor" that follows.)

Do you fear being viewed as "soft" because you really *prefer* to be seen as "hard"? Do you prefer to be considered "difficult"? What would happen if you concerned yourself a lot less with how you are viewed and much more about how you bring out the best in others?

Greater openness results in greater candor.

When I was chairman of Florida's State Board of Independent Colleges and Universities, Dr. Wayne Freeburg was our executive director. As the chairman, I was responsible for his review and, ultimately, his career advancement. I would have thought that because of our open relationship it would be difficult to do that. To the contrary, it was easier.

When you build a relationship at work on truthful communication, the fear of being candid isn't there. Candor is normal. You and your associate have built a trust that is rooted in putting each other's interest first. It actually makes reviewing an employee's work more transparent.

The reason most of us are hesitant to open up to others is that we fear they might discover the "real" us! By being open to learning about my team and what makes them tick I might have to let them learn about who I really am.

Be careful. By being a manager who constantly looks into the mirror you will always be on your guard to protect yourself first. Ironically, that's the very thing that will lead to your demise as a leader.

My early failures as a leader were rooted in "self-protection." And I wasn't alone. Some leaders hide behind being tough and all business. Other managers cover their insecurity by being aloof and above it all.

But when you become a manager who leads by opening the window between you and your team, you will discover the secret to bringing out the best in others—getting to know *them* first! No excuses; only the courage to build relationships with the people you are counting on the most.

WRAP THE GIFT
it's your newfound confidence.

What would it mean to your career if your associates could routinely make statements similar to the ones listed below?

"I can say anything to my boss without him losing his cool."

"My boss values my opinion; she asks for it all the time."

"He is so supportive of me I don't want to disappoint him."

When you choose to take the initiative and open up to your associates, that is perceived as strength. And the very thing you feared, honest give-and-take with your employee, is what creates trust almost immediately!

During my first years as a manager, I foolishly thought I had to be viewed as having all the answers. I didn't see the need to really get to know my employees; the surface information was enough upon which to base my decisions.

Consequently, their trust in my decisions was limited. And the wisdom I needed to motivate them was weak.

But that changed while I was chairing the State Board of Independent Colleges and Universities. By that time I had learned to suspend judgment and avoid making a quick decision without hearing from the entire team. I didn't want to repeat the mistake of having a head full of my own ideas and little room for anyone else's input.

For instance, one private college we examined for licensure renewal was in trouble with the U.S. Department of Education. My staff had reason to believe that the FBI was closing in on them as well. I was inclined to find a quick resolution, but my executive director and others encouraged me to travel to the college to get the facts and then go to Washington and meet one-on-one with the Department of Education personnel. In other words, hold off forming an opinion until I had listened to everyone.

I followed their lead, and it paid off. The openness I created at the college, state, and national levels helped us mediate a resolution that was in the best interest of the 10,000-plus students enrolled. I was learning to listen to our team first and thereafter to craft a solution with them.

To my surprise, staff members started sharing information with me much more freely. And I didn't sense they were holding anything back or that they were only sharing what they thought I wanted to hear. That led to a further change in me. The old stress of trying to figure out what needed to be done next gave way to a confidence that the team and I could face any situation and, by working together, make a good decision.

There is no longer an excuse for not promoting openness with your team at work. Openness improves morale, encourages more honest communication, and promotes problem solving rather than problem avoidance.

You can quickly measure a leader's openness with his associates by learning what the associates say when the leader isn't present. Banther Consulting Corporation has used our proprietary All Employee Surveys, Listening Sessions, and 360 Feedback with more than 70 percent of our client companies to provide the data necessary to prove to leaders the value of being open with others. In every case, their associates wanted and valued their openness.

The poet Ralph Waldo Emerson wrote, "Who you are speaks so loudly I cannot hear what you say!"[7] And that's why genuine and lasting leadership is more about who we have become than simply something we do. But it begins with the choices we make every day.

When you choose to become open and do so consistently, you have set the stage for actually practicing openness. No one will accuse you of just trying the "next new thing." On the contrary, your actions will provide a very clear backdrop of how much you value the people who report to you.

GIVE THE GIFT
it's your actions, not your intentions.

Life is full of awkward moments. Like the first time you asked someone on a date or someone approached you and asked you out. How about meeting your spouse's parents for the first time? Some great movies have been made about those experiences!

Work is no different. As in life, those awkward moments will be better if we have thought about what is going to happen and how we plan to approach the conversation. This is doubly true at in the workplace.

If you are going to become a boss who is open to your associates, you have to have a plan, and you must have the discipline to stick with it. Your plan for giving the gift of openness comprises three simple rules.

Rule #1: Give first.

Don't wait for your employees to seek you out. Choose to be assertive and go to them first. Have a conversation over coffee or lunch. It doesn't have to be long, but it does have to be consistent. You don't create openness in one meeting; it evolves over months as a result of continued conversations.

While you are at it, don't restrict your openness to just your employees. Why not begin to open up to associates from other departments, vendors, or even customers? Remember, you are trying to build a relationship that will result in influence. And influence is your most valued currency in the marketplace.

One of my clients is a leader in acute care facilities, with seventy hospitals in fifteen states. I was coaching the new director of one of the more troubled units in one of those hospitals. She had been brought in to lead a department that by every definition was dysfunctional, and the staff had lost their way.

We decided that she should have a few weeks to get her bearings before we would talk about how she could begin to change the culture and improve the unit's performance. Having some knowledge of this unit's history, I took a deep breath before calling to set up our first appointment, fearing she might not still be there.

Not only was she still there, she had already begun to make steady improvements. And without any coaching from me! How did she do it? She described how she had just opened herself up to every associate.

For example, a nurse called her in the middle of the night with a problem, and the new director promptly got dressed and went in to help. In fact, in the first 60 days in her new leadership position she spent more time on the floor with her staff than in her office. She wasn't there doing the work; she was there supporting her team and learning about them.

The new director didn't wait for her staff to open up to her. She didn't wait for them to get to know her. She gave first. She gave openness to everyone who came across her path, and the results were immediate!

Rule #2: Give freely.

When you are open only when you need something, you will get caught! To become an effective leader you have to be willing to create openness with every member of your team as a minimum—not just your favorites. And it's imperative that you do this as a matter of habit.

I learned firsthand the importance of giving freely to everyone you come into contact with.

I was flying from Tampa to Los Angeles to lead a focus group session at a gathering of Meeting Planners International. I was able to book a nonstop on a Sunday afternoon, and because coach was overbooked I was one of the lucky frequent flyers who got bumped up to first class.

I took my seat next to the window and thought to myself, if I don't speak to the person next to me I can take a long afternoon nap! I hardly noticed the woman who sat down beside me.

About an hour out of LA I started thinking about the topic of my focus group. Since I would be encouraging people to be more open to the people they work with, I probably should speak to my seatmate.

I turned and asked a few questions about her. We quickly realized we had a lot in common. We both had a teenage son (I had two), and we both had mothers who were elderly and needed care, mine in North Carolina and hers in Florida. Before long we were exchanging family stories.

A flight attendant interrupted us and said, "Ms. Wagner, someone in the back would like your autograph." It turns out she was Paula Wagner, of Cruise/Wagner (as in Tom Cruise) Productions!

Before I could say anything, she asked me if I had seen *Mission Impossible 1* and *2*. I replied that I had, and she wanted to know which one I liked best.

After we talked for a moment about the movies, she asked me what I did. I told her I was a management consultant who helped companies with communication and leadership. She began to describe a problem they were having on the film *Others*, starring Nicole Kidman. I described how I thought I could help. And then she asked for my card. Thank you, Delta Airlines, for bumping me up! But what if I had remained closed and chosen not to speak to Ms. Wagner? Or worse, what if the moment she sat down I had handed her my business card and started "selling." Either would have been a tragic error.

How many times is a great opportunity sitting in the seat next to us and we miss it because we are so focused on ourselves? That lesson taught me to give the gift of openness freely to everyone. (I am pleased to tell you that by focusing on my seatmates first I have walked off many flights with a cell phone number, an email address, and occasionally a contract for work!)

Now, some people will not respond. That's okay. Don't press the matter; just move on. At least you will not miss on the ones who are ready to build a profitable relationship. And if they are employees, knowing the difference will be very helpful to you as you lead them.

Rule #3: Give frequently.

If the people whom you lead are the most expensive asset your company has, then being open with them and gaining their trust is as important as any spreadsheet on your desk.

When I began to turn my leadership around, I intentionally spent time out of my office with others, being open to them for hours at a time. Amazingly, I got more work done and realized better results. Especially for those of you who are leading an enterprise that expects you to be a rainmaker, opening yourself up to people and putting their interests first is essential.

Regarding my employees, I developed a more pointed approach to creating openness. And I found this intentional effort much more useful. I developed 21 questions I wanted to ask. My list is loosely based on Harvey Mackay's work, *Dig Your Well Before You Get Thirsty*, which inspired me to create a specific list of things I wanted to know that would help me lead in a way that worked for my team and for me. Mackay referred to his list as the "Mackay 66." I call mine the "Banther 21" (or simply B-21) for the 21 things about any employee that are important for me to know.

Here is my list and how I used the answers to become a better leader:

DIGGING YOUR WELL (B21)	
QUESTION	IMPLICATION
1. Where did you grow up?	Their cultural perspective
2. What were you like as a kid?	Their early interests and habits
3. What did you do in high school?	Their natural inclinations
4. What were your early jobs?	Their first work environment
5. What happened after high school?	Their education or job pursuits
6. What did you dream of doing?	Their earliest goals and aspirations

QUESTION	IMPLICATION
7. What was an early disappointment?	Their earliest fears and doubts
8. What was an early success?	Their earliest confidence source
9. What were your first real jobs like?	Their work habit influences
10. What did you like best in those jobs?	What comes easiest too them
11. What were your first bosses like?	What impression they have of leaders
12. If you could, what would you do over?	What is an important goal still
13. What's your family like?	What matters and motivates them most
14. What hobbies do you have now?	What they use to de-stress from work
15. What's on your bucket list?	What motivates them for the future
16. What do you worry about?	What takes their focus away daily
17. What attracted you to our company?	What they look for at work
18. What do you dislike most about work?	What de-motivates them
19. What do you like best about work?	What motivates them
20. If you could do another job at work?	What attracts their attention
21. What is your most personal goal?	What matters most today to them

I don't ask all of these questions at once like an interrogation. In fact, I usually don't ask the question per se. By having regular conversations with folks and being open to them, you will find that they get around to telling you these things in the natural course of events. And within six months of their hiring, you should know these things about every employee on your team.

I do keep private notes, however. You might be thinking, "That's snooping!" I used to think that too, but if the most valuable asset in a leader's work life is a person, why wouldn't you want to make sure you paid attention to everything that was important to them? Without a few notes you will forget. When we forget about others, do you know who takes up our brain space? Ourselves! And that is dangerous.

When I am thinking about how to motivate or lead an associate, I review the implications of what I learned from their answers to my list of questions (whether asked directly or indirectly). This keeps me focused on them and how to help them achieve their goals. By extension, that means they are going to be looking for a chance to help me achieve mine.

Once I have made my initial investment in our relationship I don't think about the B-21 much. The B-21 gets me started and keeps me focused. Thereafter, we are open with and learn from each other daily. The new relationship I have developed keeps me motivated.

RECEIVE THE GIFT OF THANKS IN RETURN.

Sometimes a thank-you comes from the most unusual place. For instance, I opened up an email one night even though I didn't immediately recognize the sender's name. Turns out the sender and I worked at a three-room radio station in rural west Georgia when he was a young college student and I was "just a little bit older" than he. I had a little more experience than he did, so it was my job to train him. We couldn't have worked together more than a few months, but he wanted to thank me for being so open with him and helping him get started.

And he wanted to tell me how his life had turned out. His career had been stellar. He was inducted into the Country Music Radio DJ Hall of Fame in Nashville. He had gone back to college and was completing a master's degree. That was far more thanks (and credit) than I deserved!

When a boss gives us even the slightest hint that he accepts us and wants only the best for us, it lights an eternal flame inside. And we will work very hard to repay his trust by living up to his belief in us.

Lasting leaders can see it in our eyes. We want them to know that they were right when they took a chance on us. In fact, we will usually credit our leaders with far more than they expected.

That's what Mike Pender, a CPA in Sarasota, Florida, did. He and his partner, Steve Spangler, CPA, had worked for more than three decades in one firm when the firm's founder retired. Mike and Steve weren't far from retirement age themselves, but they had no intention of stepping aside. They had faithfully served the firm's founder, and now it was their turn to lead from the helm.

Openness to the staff had not been a prominent theme at the firm. Should they just carry on with the status quo for a few years and then sell out? Should they even think about taking a different approach and involving the other professionals and staff who now worked only for them?

Mike and Steve took the risk and brought their entire team together and, for the first time, asked some simple questions. What do we do well here? What are we missing? How could we improve? What ideas do you guys have? They both listened. And they asked more questions. In a matter of months, they began to harness the ideas and enthusiasm of their associates. They added two new partners and developed regional and national partnerships with allied businesses to offer a much broader range of financial services to their clients.

Mike and Steve have grown the firm both in the number of clients it has and in revenue. The staff have shown their thanks through their support of the firm's planning process and their willingness to be more involved. Now the two men are focused on growth and profit rather than retirement.

It's never too late to open up and invite the people who work for you to start working with you. Nothing creates a sense of ownership in employees more than treating them like owners!

It's easy to give lip service to that idea. It's become popular to "empower" employees and to invite them to "engage" in your enterprise. But those come dangerously close to the old "flavor of the month" motivational techniques and programs that have little shelf life. And managers who try to motivate

People are the bottom line.

Leaders who ignore the complete human side of those they manage will discover a team unwilling to take risks. In the past these employees might have taken risks, failed, and been blamed. And recently they have watched friends and others lose their jobs and even their homes through economic burdens that aren't due to their actions directly. Change and risk are no longer on the agenda of today's workforce. But in the current global market those are the very two things—an openness to change and a willingness to take risks—that a successful leader needs from her team.

Can you really afford not to have a strong and dedicated team that is open to change and trusts you with managing risk? No, you can't, because the bottom line is that people—the ones you are now managing—are the bottom line of your business. You will not be profitable without them. And you will not succeed as a leader in spite of them.

When I rushed off to live my dream as a manager, I had never heard of investing in your team first. And I had never heard of Nathaniel Branden, Ph.D. But he would play a big part in showing

employees only to manipulate performance will be ineffective. (See the box titled "People are the bottom line" later in this chapter.)

When you show a genuine interest in team members and open up to them, however, empowerment and engagement are the by-products. That's because trust is the required element in having employees who are willing to take risks and who will show you gratitude. By the time I opened my consulting practice, I knew I had to start by being open to my team. On the recommendation of a friend, I hired Bev Costa to be my assistant. I made an effort every day to communicate openly and show an interest in her life and her family. The reward was all mine. Her family became important to me, and me where I failed as a leader and lighting the path that eventually led me to success. Branden has spent his life researching the effect that our self-image has on our work performance. He sums up his research in one paragraph: "The policies [at work] that support self-esteem are also the policies that make money. The policies that demean self-esteem are the policies that sooner or later cause a company to lose money—simply because, when you treat people badly and disrespectfully, you cannot possibly hope to get their best. And in today's fiercely competitive, rapidly changing global economy, nothing less than their best is good enough."[8]

Before you excuse yourself from this discussion because you are never disrespectful, I want you to be a bit more honest with yourself. Disrespect is not just what we might say or do; it can also be what we don't say and what we choose not to do.

In my early management career, no one would have said that I overtly treated him or her with disrespect. But it was what I didn't say and the actions I should have taken that I didn't that sent a simple message to my staff. And the message was that I really couldn't be trusted to act in the best interest of my team.

we celebrated each time she had a new grandchild. Likewise, Bev would look out for my best interests when I was on the road with a client and unable to give my immediate input. I had never trusted someone with that before, but this time my leadership was going to be different.

Nothing creates a sense of ownership in employees more than treating them like owners.

Bev stayed with me and by my side for almost 19 years! Prior to that I had never had an assistant for longer than a few years. And when she retired, her comments about how she felt about working with me and our team thrilled me. Our working relationship was successful because it began with openness—the glue for lasting teamwork!

An even bigger thank-you can come from your clients or customers. The ability to create openness with your associates gives you the confidence to develop the same relationship with those you serve.

Being thanked by grateful clients is what Jim Couchenour had come to expect. Jim founded Cogun, Inc., one of America's premier builders of churches, whose mission is simply "to provide the greatest value of service possible in creating shelter for worship and ministry." His sons had followed him in the business, and their reputation of quality was well deserved.

But one of their clients was having serious difficulty with the project. Part of the problem resulted from mistakes made by Cogun, but the greater share stemmed from actions the church had taken that adversely impacted the construction. Jim could have instructed his managers to enforce the contract, but he and his family had built the business on openness with each other and they extended this gift of openness to their clients (or, as they preferred to call them, VSPs).

He traveled to the construction site and met personally with the church leaders on the project. He listened to their complaints and invited them to share all of their concerns. He didn't use the time to defend his company or blame the church leaders for the mistakes they had made. He chose, instead, to be open to the client and simply hear their story.

That openness resulted in a client whose thank-you will be a referral to others describing how Cogun delivered on the service even when it cost them to do so—because they are dedicated to openness and candor with their clients.

Isn't that what you want someone with a complaint to experience? Cogun has built hundreds of churches and has success stories from coast to coast. But their real strength lies in the humility to put the interests of a client on a par with their own.

Go ahead and open your door and let your associates know it. Just make sure that you open your heart and your mind at the same time. It's not the open door that is the key to building great people.

The key is being a leader who is no longer bound by prejudices and personal insecurities. A leader who knows that the best ideas often come from the average men and women who make up their team. And because the leader has become someone who offers the gift of openness to others, those average people are drawn together to create above-average results.

CHAPTER 4

THE GIFT OF INVESTING TIME IN OTHERS

"I want to see *you* grow!"

· ·

Which do you want more of, time or money? Had to think for a moment, didn't you? The answer is obvious, though: most of us would want more time. Especially for those moments we value most.

Just ask the young bride who said good-bye to her soldier husband as he deployed, the business traveler who missed his plane by seconds, or the family gathered around a beloved grandfather's hospital bed. If we could just have a few more minutes. But we can't create any more time; we can only choose how to spend the time we have.

· ·

FIND THE GIFT
it's inside you!

As a young manager I wasted so much of my time—and, as a consequence, so much of my life—on myself, foolishly thinking I had to figure out the answers, write the plan, and implement each step. It took me a while, but I

Lasting relationships require time.

During my tenure as the president of Trinity College of Florida, we began building a new campus and, as a result, faced a lot of legal issues. A young attorney in Tampa, Mark Merrill, was recommended to me. We met, I was impressed, and he was hired!

Earlier in my career I would have spent just enough time with an attorney to lay out our plan before moving on. But, from the beginning, I chose to invest more time in my professional relationship with Mark than I had with others in the past. We met regularly, and I made the decision to get to know him personally, not just in terms of what he could do for the college. Together we faced tough battles on behalf of Trinity, from zoning to regional land-use challenges.

What I didn't fully realize at the time was that this investment of my time would pay high dividends: Mark and I have enjoyed a working and personal relationship for 25 years!

learned that when we choose to consistently invest time in the people around us, listening to their ideas and their plans, that's not wasted. Instead, our time is leveraged and our influence grows greater.

Our lives aren't made up of weeks or months of activity. They are made up of moments that are a gift. And when we choose to give those moments to others, we are giving a precious part of ourselves. At times we need moments to ourselves to think and reflect. But we also need moments with our associates if we expect to build any sense of team.

We can't create any more time;
we can only choose how to
spend the time we have.

> Mark eventually stepped aside from his law practice and dedicated himself to found, with his wife, Susan, Family First, one of the foremost advocates for families and children in America. Family First is the parent organization for All Pro Dad, a program that features former Super Bowl head coach Tony Dungy and a host of athletes who encourage dads to become better fathers, and iMOM, a program led by Susan Merrill and Lauren Dungy, which does the same for mothers.
>
> Mark asked me to continue to advise him and his new organization, and that has been one of the most rewarding efforts of my professional life.
>
> Whenever I am tempted to invest the minimum amount of time with an associate, I think about how much I now value my relationship with Mark Merrill and his team. How easy it would have been to miss this opportunity if I hadn't invested in our relationship. Lasting leaders value relationships by giving of their time, and that makes a difference—for a lifetime!

Leaders are usually not solo inventors or lonely creative thinkers. We are called to assemble a team of people and enable them to be more productive together than any of them could be alone. We can't create time, but when we invest our time to build profitable relationships, we do multiply the effect of our time.

Thousands of business leaders look to Brian Tracy, author of more than 45 books for business leaders that have been translated into dozens of languages, for advice every day on how to maximize the effect of their time. His constant suggestion as a consultant to top business leaders for the past three-plus decades has been this: "Perhaps the very best question that you can memorize and repeat, over and over, is, what is the most valuable use of my time right now?"[1]

As we age, the issue of how we use our time becomes even more important to us. Which do we want in our later years, success or more time? Jane Brody, in an article on aging for the *New York Times,* reported on the work of Karl Pillemer, professor of human development at the College of Human Ecology at Cornell and a gerontologist at the Weil Cornell Medical College, who found the answer to that question by interviewing a thousand older Americans from varying backgrounds. "Not one person in a thousand said that happiness is accrued from working as hard as you can to make money to buy whatever you want."[2]

Overwhelmingly the seniors in Pillemer's study pointed out that life was too short to waste. Thomas Watson, founder of IBM, put it this way: "Wisdom is the power to put our time and our knowledge to proper use."[3]

So, with time as your most valuable possession, what's the proper use of it at work? To help you better answer that question, consider this related question: Which one of these will result in you better understanding the strengths of your team, other leaders' opinions or the actual time you are engaged with your team members learning about them?

> We can't create time, but when we invest
> our time to build profitable relationships,
> we do multiply the effect of our time.

I am constantly surprised how many leaders choose to listen first to the opinion of another leader. For example, the head of an international distribution company was describing to me the problem he was having with his team's performance. When I asked him how his team had responded when he spoke to them about this problem, he replied: "Oh, I don't have to talk to them. The VP of sales told me what he had heard they had been saying out on the shop floor." I thought, Really? You are willing to act on information you've received thirdhand?

The first gift we have to give as leaders is the gift of openness, making a conscious decision to get to know and understand everyone who works on our team. But in order to do that we have to be willing to invest enough time to do so. Just thinking about being open is not enough. Asking other people what they think about our management teams and employees is misguided. We have to be willing to give the gift of our time to those we are leading if we ever expect them to experience the companion gift of openness from us.

BUY INTO THE GIFT
it's a matter of choice!

So why don't more leaders make the choice to spend more time with their associates? After more than 25 years of advising businesses and organizations, I can say without hesitancy that the pressure to chose otherwise is usually built into the system your leaders work in.

Invest your time well and you earn a return that keeps multiplying—for a lifetime. Yet even though the benefit of a wise investment is obvious, it's not easy to implement. So many daily pressures compete for our attention. And it starts with the company culture that promotes from within. A good salesperson becomes the sales manager. A good financial analyst becomes the chief accountant. In other words, be a good "doer" and you can become the leader of other "doers."

Most of the people who are promoted to positions of management because they are great doers are smart; they're driven to perform; they put up strong results. Isn't that enough to qualify them automatically for leadership? Doesn't that mean they will naturally know how to create collaboration and team-work? No, it isn't, and no, it doesn't! In fact, without a team that is willing to follow them, these doer-leaders will have difficulty reaching or sustaining great numbers.

The problem is that when good doers become leaders they often look for things to do. And, if they are not careful, they will find something. What they find will distract their attention away from spending time with their team. It will feed their need to be doing something so that at the end of the day they can point to work accomplished. Just spending time with associates getting

Beware of time wasters
masquerading as urgent tasks!

Poring over reports first thing every morning after work has begun.

A better approach would be to review reports with key associates affected by the data so you can develop a collective response.

Making critical decisions without getting input from your team first.

No one leader has all the information necessary to make a decision. When you spend time with your team considering the decision, then you will have a greater chance of reaching the best conclusion, even if you make the final decision alone.

Going to your team after you have made a critical decision and getting their opinion.

What associates are going to risk disagreeing with the brilliant thinking their boss did alone to reach this decision? You are creating "rubber stamps" who will fail you just when you need them the most. Make decisions with your team's input and you have built a "think tank."

Meeting with other leaders to evaluate your team.

Other leaders can give you their opinions, but if you want data based on firsthand input, invest a lot of time in your team so that their performance is never a surprise to you.

Hearing about a success of or a conflict within your team and ignoring it.

No one, absolutely no one, has more influence in spreading success like a virus or containing conflict like a mother bear than you do as a leader! Engaging in both of these situations is among the most valuable time you will ever spend with your associates.

to know them, coach them, or even motivate them is hard to quantify; and for good doers, quantifying their work is everything!

Over the years, I have observed at least five top ways that leaders distract themselves from their most important work—namely, being open with and listening to their people. It's a tricky list, because at first glance these seem like important tasks. And they are. But when they replace spending time with your team, these tasks have little lasting value.

At this point you might be thinking, "Hold on, Barry. I spend time with my associates every year at our Christmas party and our summer picnic, and I even try to get everybody together once a month!" Well, that's a start, but your return will be minimal.

Think of it like saving or investing money. The key is the power of compounding. Investing a small amount of money consistently over a long period of time will yield a greater return than large amounts of money over a shorter period.

The same is true with time invested in others. Choosing to invest a few minutes every day will yield a greater return than will several hours of time every few months. Tom Peters labeled this as "management by wandering around,"[4] and he suggested that good leaders are *constantly* walking around and observing employees at work.

I would add the encouragement that you stop and take a few minutes with each associate as you're walking around. Use the tools we discussed in the previous gift of openness to deepen your relationships as you go! A little bit of time every day will be far more effective than a block of hours only now and again.

One of the biggest reasons to spend more time with your associates, however, is what it will do for *you*. Obsessing in your office can become paralyzing. But time spent with your team will be invigorating for you and them. (See the box that follows, which describes a successful steel company that was built on the foundation of a leader pouring his heart into his employees.)

Choosing to invest your time in the people you lead so that you can become more aware of who they are, what motivates them, and what challenges they

A steel company can have a heart.

Buck McInnis borrowed all the money he could and purchased a business called Tampa Bay Steel. It was a company he had recently been fired from! He spent the next 25 years building a company rooted in strong customer service and employee relationships. A natural salesman, Buck invested a lot of time in prospects and customers. But he also spent time with his employees.

Tampa Bay Steel grew beyond anything Buck could imagine. But one thing has not changed: He still spends time with his management team and on the manufacturing plant floor with the hourly guys who bend and shape the steel. Ask him the business he is in and you won't hear a pitch about steel. You will hear about employees, by name, and the relationship he has built with them over decades.

Buck was managing by walking around long before Tom Peters wrote about it!

I have heard him say over and over, "When I talk to employees it inspires me; gosh, we have a great team!" That respect and appreciation is mutual: there has been very little turnover in the past decade at Tampa Bay Steel. And those employees will tell you they feel like Buck is still as close to them as the day they started.

face is the hallmark of successful and lasting leaders. Often, though, when I talk with my clients' employees, I find the opposite. More than 50 percent of the time when I ask a person to "tell me about the time your boss spends with you," I get a snicker, a laugh, or a "what time?"

"The only time I spend with my boss is when he calls us into the conference room and reams us out because he just got yelled at by the president." That was how a supervisor in one of the country's largest healthcare plan management companies answered my simple question. The company was in deep trouble, and I had been retained to try to solve their employee morale and retention problems. My first surprise was that they considered these two separate challenges!

When I interviewed the bosses, it became clearer what was going on. Their solution to the drop in morale was simply to fire the current group and bring in another team. All with little regard to the $10,000 to $15,000 in hard costs they would lose with each turnover. I further asked one of them what role the team played in helping to set the performance goals that everyone seemed to be missing, and she lamented: "I have to set these goals; my team can't be trusted with that. I am responsible for hitting those targets!"

Upper leadership is panicking at missed targets. Managers are trying to coerce better performance from their team. The team feels ignored and unappreciated. And on top of all of this, no one, at any level, is having extended conversations vertically throughout the company to find out what is going on!

To do that work they hired an outside consultant. Hiring any outsider was expensive because it absolutely wouldn't have been necessary in the first place if a lasting leader had emerged who shared the gift of investing time in the staff at all levels. But I can't be too hard on them because their situation in business is not unique. In fact, *Forbes* magazine recently corroborated my findings in their own broad survey of corporate employees, through which they found that:

> More than 30% believe they'll be working someplace else in twelve months.
>
> More than 40% don't respect the person they report to.
>
> More than 50% say they have different values than their employer.
>
> More than 60% don't feel that their career goals align with their employer's.
>
> More than 70% don't feel appreciated or valued by their employer.[5]

I have never worked with a leader who regretted the time he or she chose to invest in the associates at all levels of the company. But I have counseled dozens who told me: "I wish I had spent more time with my team listening [or sharing or getting their input or asking for ideas]." The good news is that you get to choose which group you will become a part of, starting today!

WRAP THE GIFT
it's yours to prioritize.

There can be only one conclusion. Should you decide you want to give the gift of your time to your associates, you have to wrap your mind around an entirely new paradigm. Simply put, you have to believe that you can make no better investment of the limited time you have than to spend it with the people you lead.

Each day when you are walking into work or heading to a meeting and you pass an employee, stop and give that person 60 seconds. Ask one question and listen. After awhile you will get pretty good at measuring out 60 seconds in your head. And, more importantly, you will be building a relationship of paying attention to the people you are depending on. Go to www.aleaders gift.com, click on the "Gift of Time" tab, and complete an exercise that will reveal the power of 60 seconds in your life.

The number-one reason employees voluntarily leave an employer in the first 18 to 24 months after being hired is the lack of coaching. Ashland, Inc., (see the box titled "Prioritize your time.") and other profitable proactive companies beat that average by expecting managers to spend time with associates: getting to know them, helping them understand company goals and objectives, and enabling them to create their own accomplishments.

Time invested by you with the people you lead pays! I have seen this truth work for dozens of clients, one of them being the healthcare plan management company I described earlier. They took my advice and chose to have their leaders invest time in their teams: They listened to them. They got to know them. They coached them. They learned from one another and planned together.

The chairman wrote and thanked me, saying, "We are growing at

Prioritize your time.

Prioritizing your time is more of a choice than it is a skill.

James O'Brien made that choice in his role as a leader and eventually chairman at Ashland, Inc., which began in 1924 as a small oil refinery in the hills of eastern Kentucky. As the company grew through the first half of the twentieth century, it faced stiff competitive forces. But O'Brien believed, "You have to get people to truly understand what you are trying to do."[6]

The only way for his people to understand that, of course, was for him to invest enough time with his staff so that they not only heard what he had to say but also saw and started to understand what he was trying to accomplish at Ashland. One core company value is to encourage managers to connect with employees regularly. That means time!

By the first decade of the twenty-first century that philosophy was paying off—in a big way! Today Ashland is in more than 100 countries and is known as a Fortune 500 manufacturer of chemicals, plastics, motor oil, and other specialized products and services.

"People development is the foundation for all the other core elements of our culture," says O'Brien. "We believe the legacy we leave as a company will not be in our business accomplishments. It will be in our people and their accomplishments."[7]

10 percent a month and our turnover is 25 percent of what it was . . . quite simply [you] did an outstanding job." I didn't do it, they did. And you can too when you see your time as a gift and you freely give it to the people you lead. Then they will give you the business results you are looking for.

Make the choice to spend more specific time with your associates and you will have some extraordinary research to stand on. Jim Trinka, PhD, was the chief learning officer for the FBI when he gathered the most relevant data on this issue. His study of thousands of manager-employee surveys in government and industry led to startling results. Trinka concluded that by focusing on "developing others" and "communication" competencies, managers can increase their overall leadership effectiveness "by 50–60 percent"![8]

The research further suggested that the most valuable development and communication managers could do was immediate. In other words, daily—not once a year! "A vast majority of employees want someone at work [usually their managers] to conduct dialogues on performance, mission importance and alignment," Trinka reported.[9]

In his study Trinka references Frank LaFasto and Carl Larson's *When Teams Work Best*, which revealed that businesses with "top tier" leadership qualities outperform their competitors in revenue margins by better than 500 percent and in net income by 700 percent! The 6,000 team members they surveyed defined one of those key leadership qualities as "Ensures a Collaborative Climate." "The team leader must ensure a climate that enables team members to speak up and address the real issues preventing the goals from being achieved," asserted the authors.[10]

These kinds of results, however, come only to those leaders who prioritize their time so they invest daily in the people they lead. Are you ready to practice what the hundreds of successful leaders I have advised and coached do to prioritize their time? Make the personal choice to do it and read on!

GIVE THE GIFT
it's your actions, not your intentions.

"Whatever gets measured gets done!" It's hard to pin down who said this. Drucker? Peters? Deming? Regardless of who said it first, it works! And most of us accept that it holds true about daily work tasks.

But are we willing to measure the "softer" side of working and leading? Would you be willing to keep a spreadsheet on the amount of time you spend with each of your associates to ensure that you are making an adequate investment? If you believe this time spent is like any other investment, then you will have no trouble motivating yourself to create this spreadsheet and start measuring time with your team. Because what gets measured gets done!

I have learned through my clients and by managing my own professional services firm that there are three distinct segments of time you have to plan for, measure, and evaluate. Track your time with each associate just like you would an investment.

1. The employees who report to you need time daily. Make sure you spend 60 seconds with every one of your direct reports. Vary your pattern—don't make it seem like a ritual. Just make sure every associate gets at least that much time with you daily. This is not meeting time or customer review time. This is time where you are listening to each individual. It can be either personal or professional.

2. Your direct reports need time every week. Based on the number, this can be between fifteen and thirty minutes. It can be over lunch. It can be in your office or theirs. But it needs to be one-on-one for up to half an hour. Should you have direct reports who are geographically dispersed then do these sessions by phone or tele-call (Skype, etc.). But do them.

3. Your direct reports need time monthly. Invest 1 hour—just sixty minutes— each month in everyone who reports to you. I can hear the push back. "Barry, I have ten direct reports. Are you telling me I have to spend ten hours a month investing in these men and women?!" Yes, that is exactly what I am saying.

4. You will either spend that one hour a month now, or you will spend multiple hours later on when you're trying to fix a problem that could have been avoided if you'd invested in your direct reports. Or when you're trying to get their replacement(s) up to speed when the predecessor failed from lack of attention.

5. Don't fudge and count group meetings or spontaneous discussions about customer issues as these interactions. This is you and your employees' one-on-one. And each interaction should be a broad conversation with you mostly doing the listening, not the speaking.

You don't have to change the oil in your car every 3,000 miles, but when you don't, the negligence will eventually catch up with you—and it will cost a lot more than a quart or two of motor oil. If you don't invest time in your associates, it is a double loss: One, you lose their engagement and loyalty. And when they quit (or worse yet, when they quit but don't leave), you will lose their ideas, their input, and their effort.

Now you might be asking what you are to do with all the information you are getting from time spent with your team. I have observed that successful leaders always ask themselves three questions after each encounter.

What did I learn?

What action, if any, do I need to take?

What do I need to cover in the future with this associate?

Asking these questions as the result of regular and consistent interaction is the foundation of a culture where employees feel safe to communicate freely. That means you will hear about problems sooner and solutions will not be delayed. But without measuring it, this will be difficult to accomplish.

A contemporary business leader has spoken out on the value of such measurement. No stranger to logic or analytics, Bill Gates was quoted in a January 2013 article in the *Wall Street Journal*: "In the past year, I have been struck by how important measurement is to improving the human condition. You can achieve incredible progress if you set a clear goal and find a measure that will drive progress toward that goal . . ."[11]

So, I am going to suggest a new mantra. "What is valued gets measured." Giving the gift of time is worthy of our attention, our measurement, and our progress if we expect to create a collaborative environment of success.

What is valued gets measured.

RECEIVE THE GIFT OF THANKS IN RETURN.

The ancient writer of the book of Ephesians in the New Testament put it this way: "Be careful how you live, not as unwise men but as wise, making the most of your time . . ."[12] When other people value the time you gave them far more than you thought they would, that's a good sign that you have invested wisely!

There are 1,440 minutes in every day. It's the same amount for all of us. The difference is in how we choose to spend them. And the thanks we earn are the result of our choices.

Often those thanks can even be seen on the bottom line. What percentage of meaningful inventions or ideas do you think come from the rank-and-file workers in a company? Would you believe most of them? J.C. Spender and Bruce Strong, writing in the *Wall Street Journal*, concluded, "Most great ideas for enhancing corporate growth and profits aren't discovered in the lab late at night, or in the isolation of the executive suite. They come from the people who daily fight the company's battles, who serve the customers . . . in other words the employees."[13]

Johnson and Johnson, Wal-Mart, and 3M are all companies that encourage employees to think about improving products and processes, and they expect leaders to invest time in associates to unleash those ideas. (Think Band-Aid, the Wal-Mart greeter, and Scotch tape!) Their thank-you? It comes in the form of consistently rising sales and growing profit.

Time is a just a vehicle. It's the transportation source for conversations, relationships, and new ideas. And when you and I make the decision to invest time in our teams, we can expect to get a few quick thank-yous at first, and later on expressions of personal appreciation such as these (among the many

I've received since I made the transformation from a leader who was trying to *get something* to a leader who has *something to give*):

> You gave me the hope I needed at the moment I needed it most.

> Thanks for believing in me when I didn't even believe in myself.

> You have no idea how the time you gave me saved my career!

> I am who I am today because of what you did for me.

But the most significant thank-you comes in the form of the credit we receive for the good work those empowered employees do!

It's possible to be open toward others in your heart but never choose to spend any time with them. You may be prone to encouraging others, but if you don't take the time to do so you will never receive the gratitude—at any of the levels I just described—for it.

When I was nearing the end of my career in broadcasting, a young man named Mike Gonzalez applied to work in our station in Tampa. He had a voice out of central casting but practically no experience using it on radio. I had already begun my transition over to working at Trinity College of Florida when he showed up.

By that time in my career, I had trained dozens of announcers, and as VP and general manager, I certainly didn't have to do that anymore. But the letter I had received about my failure as a manager still gnawed at me now and then, so I chose to take the time to give Mike a genuine opportunity and to encourage him.

I taught him some basics about operating the equipment and how to read the program log. I also took some time to listen to his dreams about where he wanted his career to go. He was a quick study, and as a man of deep faith, he always expressed his thanks. I, too, was glad for the opportunity to be more open and to invest more in others without expecting anything in return—especially since I would be leaving the station soon.

After I left I would hear Mike on the air occasionally, and it was evident to me that he was living up to the confidence we had all placed in him. I never gave it another thought. Mike, on the other hand, never forgot it.

It has been more than 30 years since I hired Mike Gonzalez, but even now when I see him he is quick to introduce me as the "man who gave me my first job and had time for me." In fact, he has said that over the air as well. But Mike is no longer a radio announcer. He has been promoted far beyond that. He is the general manager of a CTN Network Television Station in Palm Beach, Florida.

You can't guess ahead of time which member of your team will take the time you invest in him or her and grow from it. That's why you, as the leader, have to be willing to take the risk and invest some time in *everyone you lead*. For many it may not make any lasting difference. But for some it will make all the difference in their life and they will continue to thank you for the rest of your life.

CHAPTER 5

THE GIFT OF LISTENING TO OTHERS

"I want to hear *your* ideas!"

· ·

I was busy preparing for a new class that I had to teach in an hour when the noise outside my office went from a dull roar of students dragging themselves to class to cries of "What?" "Are you sure?" "No, it couldn't have!" in a matter of seconds. I tried to stay focused on my lecture notes, but when a colleague burst through my door without knocking, I realized something was wrong. He told me to come outside quickly.

The courtyard was full of students, faculty, and staff all looking up into the bright Floridian sunlight of a January morning. They were pointing at the white contrail of the Space Shuttle *Challenger* that had just taken off from nearby Cape Kennedy. We had seen this sight many times before, and most of us had stopped bothering to even notice the smoky aftermath of a launch. But this time it was different.

Instead of trailing off into the blue sky, the white trail was broken into pieces and falling toward earth. It was obvious that something had gone terribly wrong. We moved from the courtyard to the lobby where a television had been rolled out. Within the hour we were sharing the grief of this national tragedy. The *Challenger* had broken apart seventy-three seconds into its flight. And all seven crewmembers had died.

What happened? It seemed inconceivable to us that as successful as our recent space efforts had been that something this horrible could occur. But as the investigation unfolded, it became apparent that the problem wasn't completely technical.

It would be thirty-two months before the Space Shuttle program would resume flight. In the interim, President Ronald Reagan set up the Rogers Commission to get to the bottom of what happened. The problem wasn't at the bottom, however; it was at the top of the organization.

Engineers had warned about launching in low temperatures, and there were concerns early on about the O-ring erosion and the joints.[1] But their concerns were not passed along. Why not? Who wouldn't consider these issues critical? NASA's organizational culture and decision-making processes, it turned out, had played an important role in this tragic event.

FIND THE GIFT
it's inside you!

Of course, had officials fully realized what the engineers were saying, they would have acted differently. But when genuine *listening* is not part of your work culture, it is highly likely that you, as a leader, will miss or at least misunderstand vital information that your associates are trying to tell you.

When the shuttle flew again, NASA had worked hard to build a culture with greater openness to communication. That meant listening had to be valued—not just as a means to employee satisfaction but also as a tool for ensuring the highest quality and safety of every flight.

Without this there isn't the trust required to ensure open communication. Trust between leaders and their associates is built upon a transparency that reflects a freedom to speak and to be heard. Finding the gift of listening within you means that you have to become vulnerable. You have to choose to let the other person share not only their thoughts but also how they feel. How would your employees respond if I were to ask them if you really want to know what they are thinking? Have your listening habits built trust?

Brenda Barnes is the former CEO of the Sara Lee Corporation and, prior to that, the first female CEO of Pepsi-Cola North America. Sara Lee is a consumer goods company that has undergone significant transition since 2001 because Brenda Barnes has practiced a people-centered leadership that brings out the best in her team. Barnes is very clear that open communication with sincere listening has been at the heart of her leadership. "Bad leaders create a culture that tells them what they want to hear. Good leaders want the truth because they can fix it and capitalize on it. If people are intimidated and afraid and worried about their jobs, they fear speaking up about something that is bad. You have to create an environment that opens this up. How are you going to fix anything if you don't know about it?"[2]

> Trust between leaders and their associates is built upon a transparency that reflects a freedom to speak and be heard.

Bad culture, where listening isn't valued, impacts business every day across America. More wrong-site surgeries than we would like to know will be performed at hospitals in major cities today. Who wasn't listening? Workplace errors that will require rework to satisfy a customer will occur. Who didn't listen the first time?

The U.S. Department of Labor has reported that as much as 55 percent of a leader's work time is spent listening.[3] And surveys of corporate leaders consistently reveal that they believe listening is the most important skill in the workplace. Yet the thousands of employee surveys my firm has processed over the past two decades reveal that employees don't believe their leader is genuinely listening most of the time.

On one survey the question was asked, "If your supervisor could improve in one area that would make a difference in your work performance, what should it be?" Among the numerous cynical answers (some too rude to print) one stood out. "Value my opinion enough to look at me and listen whenever I am trying to tell you something. I could save you from a lot of trouble." When the person who leads us doesn't listen to us, we can sense it—and we don't like it.

When we suspect someone isn't listening to us, what do we typically ask? Usually it's something like, "Will you please pay attention?" Attention is defined as "the act or state of applying the mind to something."[4] So, when we are asked to pay attention, we are actually expected to pay the price of applying our mind—not our ears only—to what is being said. In other words, listening costs something. It costs the full attention of our mind.

But just think of what you will save by spending time and energy really listening to your employees!

What would it mean to your career, for instance, to have employees who were on the lookout to save you from unnecessary problems? The Rogers Commission officially reported that NASA's decision to launch the shuttle was flawed: top-level decision makers had not been informed of problems with the O-rings and joints.[5] Listening pays. And failure to listen sometimes comes at a very high price.

BUY INTO THE GIFT
it's a matter of choice!

The new president of the company stood at the front of the room and delivered his charge to his team. "Pour your whole heart into your job! The key to a great company is great employees! And I believe you are great. So I expect everyone to follow my lead and work hard and do whatever it takes to please our customers!"

Sounds like a reasonable request, doesn't it? After all, the president has cared enough to cheer the team on. But the measure of how well everyone will "put their heart into it" won't be in the number of pep rallies he holds.

To the contrary, success will be determined by how well he and his team communicate minute-by-minute, day-by-day, one-on-one. And that give-and-take must be his initiative.

Few people have researched, written, and spoken about this subject more than former Harvard Business School professor John Kotter. After decades of examining communication between leaders and employees, he came to this conclusion: "Without credible communication, and a lot of it, the hearts and minds of others are never captured."[6]

What makes communication credible? Most of us would say it is when a genuine and open exchange of ideas has occurred. That means we have moved beyond merely hearing and recognizing the sounds someone else is making. We have begun to listen. And we have expressed our ideas clearly as well.

If we aren't able to offer the gift of genuine listening, the person with whom we are speaking won't really feel valued. In fact, that employee might even feel used or disposable. What does that do to promote teamwork, collaboration, or loyalty? Nothing.

Knowing that paying attention and listening to our employees is so valuable, why don't we listen?

I frequently ask my audience of managers and executives to give me their reasons why they don't choose to fully listen. The top five responses are these:

I have something else on my mind.

I am too busy thinking about what I have to do next.

The person is taking too long to get to the point.

I have already made up my mind about what I am going to do.

I don't trust their opinion in the first place.

When you look at this list, it becomes obvious that many leaders don't value the person speaking and are more convinced that their own ideas and agenda are vastly more important. If you could read the mind of your boss the next time you met with him and could see this was his opinion of you, how would that affect your attitude? Your work performance?

When we listen, *really listen,* by setting aside all other distractions, we will not miss even the slightest piece of valuable information the person speaking might have to tell us. But if as a matter of course we choose to ignore the people speaking to us, it is highly likely that we will not pick up on those vital pieces of information. Which approach makes better sense? Which approach is more likely to produce a lasting leader with enthusiastic followers?

We don't listen sometimes because we hear so many distracting voices. Yet when we finally choose to listen to someone, we will begin to slowly turn down the volume on the noise around us and make a connection with that person, which is the foundation of winning teamwork.

We can't force anyone to feel any particular way. But our words and our actions are like a mirror in which they look to determine how they will choose to feel about themselves when they are in our presence. Maya Angelou once remarked, "I've learned that people will forget what you said, people will forget what you did, but people will never forget how you made them feel."[7] If we will let them, our employees will tell us how we make them feel.

Harvard Business Review reported on a manager at the Hanover Insurance Company who decided to ask his employees what they liked and didn't like about his leadership style. In other words, how did they feel about him and themselves? "He learned that it really bothered them when he glanced at his phone or responded to e-mail during meetings. He now refrains from those activities, and his team appreciates the change."[8] This manager learned firsthand the truth of what M. Scott Peck, author of the classic work *A Road Less Traveled*, meant when he wrote, "You cannot truly listen to anyone and do anything else at the same time."[9]

When we finally choose to listen to someone, we will begin to slowly turn down the volume around us and make a connection with that person, which is the foundation of winning teamwork.

Have you ever watched the famous vintage E.F. Hutton financial services commercials available on YouTube? The scene is always a busy setting in which a pair of executives is talking and one of them brings up that E.F. Hutton is his broker. The announcer breaks in and says, "When E.F. Hutton talks . . . "—at which point everyone else stops and turns their head toward the pair—and resumes, "*everybody* listens!"

The implication is clear. Everyone listens because they value what E.F. Hutton has to say. You and I don't often give our associates our full attention because we don't fully value what they have to say. And that could be a fatal oversight on our part.

In the two previous chapters you discovered the gift of openness—choosing to set aside preconceived notions and really getting to know the people we lead and what is important to them—and the gift of time—choosing to invest our most precious commodity in the associates we are now more open to. By doing this we are showing others that they are valuable to us. Doesn't it make sense, then, for us to use that time to genuinely listen to them?

The celebrated twentieth-century psychiatrist Karl Menninger (whose body of work earned him the Presidential Medal of Freedom) studied and examined thousands of human interactions over the course of his career. His conclusions about the unique impact of listening remain important for leaders to hear today: "Listening is a magnetic and strange thing, a creative force. The friends who listen to us are the ones we move toward. When we are listened to, it creates us, makes us unfold and expand."[10]

The very act of genuinely listening not only demonstrates our value for the one to whom we are listening but also joins us together in a relationship of mutual trust that transcends even strong differences of opinion. Go to www. aleadersgift.com and complete a personal listening assessment to see how well you are really listening to your team.

Take a "Listening Tour."

One of my most rewarding client relationships is with one of the brightest people I have ever worked with. Elliott Wiser was the corporate vice president for news and local programming for Bright House Networks. He was responsible for operations that cover the coveted I-4 corridor in central Florida from St. Petersburg to Orlando.

By all accounts Elliott is a creative genius. His approach to twenty-four-hour news and sports programming has been cutting edge and industry leading. With capable leaders at every level across three stations you would think he could rest on his laurels and simply harvest the fruit of his work. But he hasn't.

One of the important tasks he has carved out for himself is a "listening tour." He regularly visits all three stations and has only one agenda—to listen to the associates. What are they thinking? What do they need? Where does the company (including people at all levels) need to improve? (Note: This has to be done with caution. Sometimes an associate will use it as an opportunity to

WRAP THE GIFT
it has nothing to do with hearing.

Even when someone can hear us, we intuitively know whether or not they are really listening. We may show a little more patience at work than we do at home, but we still wonder whether the other person is really listening or just waiting to respond. Few people are actually listening to understand.

But when I understand that you understood what I said, then I know you "bash" his supervisor. But Elliott is seasoned enough to recognize this.)

The real payoff, however, is not just what he hears but the message he sends. When a corporate leader at this level will invest time in every associate, it tells them all that they matter and that *winning on the bottom line means developing their human potential as members of the team.*

The result has been news and sports services that have grown and prospered. Elliott is proof that the quickest and most lasting way to impact the bottom line is not through a leader's unique ideas. Rather, it comes about in his relationships—built on listening with openness and time freely given—with the people he leads. And Elliott's ability to bring out the best in people didn't go unnoticed in the marketplace. Shortly before this book was finished he was chosen to be the next president of the Gannett Television Station in the Tampa Bay market. How did he begin his first week on the job? With a listening tour, of course!

were listening to me. And there are few moments that make us feel more valued as a person than when we believe someone is genuinely listening to us.

When we are communicating in a way that enhances a person's sense of self-worth and value, then another dimension of understanding opens up to us. Peter Drucker put it this way: "The most important thing in communication is to hear what isn't being said."[11]

It's a paradox. The more we listen, really listen, to what is being said then the more we come to realize what isn't being spoken. But it requires great patience on our part to build this kind of relationship. This was a painful lesson for me to learn one evening in a conversation with my oldest son.

It actually began a few days earlier. I had decided to re-sod our lawn. First

I hired an irrigation company to put in a sprinkler system and hook it up to our town's reclaimed water system. The yard would always be watered and the price would be right.

The sod was delivered on a Friday afternoon. Early Saturday morning I started laying the sod and put the last piece in at dusk. Sunday was my legal day to water and I couldn't wait!

But early Sunday morning when I stepped out onto the porch expecting to hear the sound of the sprinkler system, I heard nothing. I went to the irrigation pump. Everything seemed okay. I couldn't call anyone until Monday morning. But the grass was still damp, so I stayed calm.

Monday morning the picture worsened. The sprinkler would not come on when I tried to override it manually, and when I called the city they informed me that the recycled water was down for repair and wouldn't be back on for a week. My sprinkler guy, who should have known this, wasn't answering the phone.

After work on Monday afternoon, I started dragging hoses across my yard and running up the bill from our regular water supply. About that time David, who was dual enrolled in high school and college, arrived home.

When he stepped out of his car, I asked, "How was class?" Being the candid 18-year-old that he was, he replied, "Not good; I did bad on an exam."

And at that moment he became my sprinkler guy and the city water manager wrapped up in one. I couldn't hear what David *wasn't* saying because I was primed to give somebody a piece of my mind!

I unloaded on him for the next five minutes. "Why didn't you study? Don't you know how important this grade is on your transcript for college?" He simply stood in the driveway staring at me and then slumped toward the front door.

In an instant I realized I had overreacted. "David, what do you want from me?" was the only question I could muster up. He stopped at the door, turned, and said to me in a very calm voice, "I would like for you to treat me with some of that stuff you teach other people to do."

I could have crawled under my precious new lawn. He was right. I wasn't listening to him. And what I should have been hearing was not what he said but what he was feeling. But I was so wrapped up in me that I couldn't hear straight!

> There are few moments that make us feel more valued as a person than when we believe someone is genuinely listening to us.

Has this ever happened to you with your children? Your spouse? How about at work with your employees? Leaders have to be able to listen to anything without losing their self-control, their self-esteem, or their self-confidence. In one conversation with my son, I lost all three!

When you are listening at work, the value is not in what you are going to say in response but in the environment you are creating. Do your employees expect you to listen first and then respond? Or do they expect you to unleash on them your pent-up emotions from the day? Whether we are trying to respond too quickly to what we are hearing or we are still rehashing our problems from earlier in the day, we can't possibly be listening to the person standing in front of us.

Drucker was right. The more you listen without trying to craft a response, the more you hear what is not being said. And that is the environment of openness that results in a more cohesive work team and a more informed leadership. These are the two critical success factors necessary to compete effectively.

Listening will lead you to hearing more. And the more you hear the more you will know. Successful managers today are not necessarily the smartest nor the hardest-working person. But they had better be the one who knows how to bring the team together and harness their energy in achieving a common goal.

That's why the gift of listening is more valuable than ever. When people are listened to, they feel valued, and when they feel valued, they trust the source of that gift. And trust is the currency of choice when leading a team.

GIVE THE GIFT
it's your actions, not your intentions.

"Lean forward . . . keep your eyes focused . . . nod your head . . . that's good!" If you have ever been to a seminar on listening you might have heard instructions such as these. If so, I'm asking you now to *please forget them!* Listening is not about a few surface physical gestures. Of course you should concentrate on the other person and not be distracted, but genuine listening that produces the kind of results I am talking about comes from far below the surface.

It is the result of a set of skills you have learned, practiced, implemented, and practiced again daily that transforms you as a leader who knows how to hear with your heart and mind and thus hear both what's being said and what's not being said. Before we examine that set of skills, though, I need to ask you a question. Are you looking for a quick fix, or are you willing to make a life change?

Let me give you an example of what I mean. As I was growing up my favorite pro golfer was Arnold Palmer. (I wasn't alone.) Several years ago I got the chance to watch him play in a senior PGA tournament. I was up before dawn and standing at the practice tee as the sun came up.

Within a few minutes The King appeared, hitching his pants and smiling at the hundreds of us already pressed up against the ropes. He bantered back and forth with Lee Trevino and Gary Player, and I realized they had done this routine for decades around the world.

When it came time to tee off, thousands of people were lining the fairway to watch Mr. Palmer, already 70-plus years of age, drive the ball around the course. He would hit a shot and everyone would applaud whether it was any good or not. And when he would make the occasional spectacular swing and place the ball near the cup, we would all erupt like it was Sunday afternoon at Augusta!

The round ended and I headed for my car already replaying the memory of a day I wouldn't forget. As I passed the practice tee I looked over, and there he was. Arnold Palmer was with a coach who probably hadn't even been born when The King won his last tournament. Palmer would hit the ball and the youngster would suggest moving his foot or completing his swing.

I stood there alone and thought, why is Palmer doing this? We don't care how he plays. He's worth a gazillion dollars; what does it matter? And then it dawned on me: that's why he's Arnold Palmer and I'm not! He was doing in his 70s what he did in his 20s—listening so he could get just a little bit better!

Are you willing to do that? Even though you already have the title of director, VP, CEO, CFO, do you believe you could still improve? This is not easy, and it requires a lifetime commitment to being aware of how you are listening and whether or not your team is willingly following you.

I had to learn the following five skills in order to be able to listen and bring out the best in people. I still work on these every day and am confident they will work for you as successfully as they have for the thousands of leaders with whom I have shared them. If you will make the commitment to start practicing these five skills, you will be surprised at how the people you lead will respond more positively and more quickly to you.

Skill #1: Stop, drop, and listen.

I would come home from Trinity College of Florida with an arm full of papers to grade and my briefcase. My young sons would come running up to me shouting, "Daddy, Daddy, Daddy!" I would shoo them away and tell them to let me put things in my office. They would become discouraged and disappear. My wife, Janice, reminded me that my older son had learned in school that in case of fire he was to stop, drop, and roll. She kindly suggested I adapt that when I came home each evening: I was to stop, drop everything, and just listen to the boys for a minute. That would be all they needed.

The next day—primarily for spite—when I walked in and David and John came running, I dropped everything, went to my knees, and just listened. I was amazed. Janice was right: it took only a minute for them to connect with me. Those sixty seconds each evening began to build a relationship that has lasted for decades.

When your employees are speaking to you, be there and nowhere else. Stop what you are doing, drop whatever you were working on, and just listen. It's the first skill in sending this message to your employees: I value you and I want to hear what you are thinking.

Let me give you another personal example. My secretary at the college came into my office one afternoon and asked if we could discuss an upcoming event. Without looking up I agreed it was important that we should. As she started to explain the circumstances, I interrupted her and said, "Why don't you put it in a memo so I can reflect on it and give you a thorough answer?"

When she didn't respond, I stopped what I was doing and looked up. She seemed startled. I asked what was wrong, and she answered me in a sharp tone. "I *did* send you a memo, you responded to it, and that's why I came in here. The last line in your memo asked me to come to your office when I was ready to go over it!"

You can't fake listening. It will catch up to you and you might end up—as I did—feeling embarrassed or humiliated. But the real cost will be in the amount of time it takes you to clean up the miscommunication you have caused along the way. Stop, drop, and listen will prevent that!

Skill #2: Suspend judgment.

You could say about me when I was a young manager that I was often wrong but never in doubt! In fact, I thought if I didn't act like I had the answer I would lose respect. I had it backward: pretending to have all the answers is the chief cause of not being respected.

When one of my team approaches me now with something, I start whispering under my breath "suspend judgment." Why do you think they call it "jumping" to a conclusion? Because you are usually taking a dangerous leap to come up with an answer so quickly!

If you are prone to snap judgments and haven't disciplined your mind to routinely suspend judgment, then you will assess, judge, and determine each of your employee's capabilities within minutes. From your assumptions you will decide how you communicate with them and even what role they will play in your organization. And you might be wrong!

We all make these kind of unwarranted assumptions. And not just at work. A few years ago I walked into my home after work one evening and my wife didn't greet me—no kiss, not even a hello. I thought to myself, I don't want the rest of the evening to go like this, so I walked into the kitchen and asked Janice if something was wrong.

She looked rather sternly at me and replied, "Yes, there is. This morning I thought about a question I wanted to ask you. I thought about what your typical response would be. And I'm mad at you for it!"

I frantically raised my hand and said, "Please, give me another shot at the question!"

You are probably laughing at this example, but we all make assumptions about someone and base our actions or maybe even long-term plans on how to work around that person. All from an assumption that might be totally unfounded!

Let me introduce you to some else who learned this the hard way. Frank is not only a client but also a good friend. And even though I had coached him on not being so "quick with an answer," it was a hard habit for him to break. After hanging up from a lengthy phone conference, he looked up from his desk and noticed that both his secretary and his intern had left their desks. Grabbing his phone he dialed the extension of one of his directors and got a voice mail.

By now this production-obsessed leader was convinced his team was goofing off with another informal office "chat." Frank decided he had had enough. Storming out of his office he started calling his secretary's name in a loud and angry tone of voice. "Linda, what are you doing to waste time now?"

When he turned the corner toward the hallway, he suddenly saw his secretary, his intern, and the director he was looking for. They were standing behind a table with a birthday cake all lit up! And around them were all the rest of the staff who were in the building that day. Just as Frank's face turned beet red his secretary spoke up in a hurt tone: "Happy Birthday, Frank!"

When you are talking with a team member, learn to hold back on your first response and make no judgment until you have exhausted your conversation with this associate. Now, that doesn't mean your first impulse might not be right, but give it just a few minutes to simmer. Even best-selling author and journalist Malcolm Gladwell, who encourages us to trust quick decisions, also reminds us, "The key to good decision making is not knowledge. It is understanding. We are swimming in the former. We are desperately lacking in the latter."[12]

You can get knowledge out of a book or from a computer screen. But understanding is the result of dialogue that is rooted in open and honest communication. Give yourself time to find understanding—suspend judgment.

Skill #3: Search deeper.

Rarely will an employee, and certainly a child or a spouse for that matter, reveal everything to you about something right off the bat. As the leader, it is your job to bring out what the other person is thinking. Learn to suspend judgment and thereafter to search deeper for what the person is trying to convey.

Using several verbal cues will help you get to these deeper meanings. Rather than responding with your opinion, ask the person follow-up questions such as these:

QUESTION	IMPLICATION
How do you mean that?	This will show how they really feel about this.
Can you give me an example?	This will describe what they are thinking.
Why is this important?	This will reveal how serious they are about this.
How will this affect us?	This will measure the cost.

You may already know the answers to these questions, but when you invite your employees' responses, you are discovering whether or not they know the answers. That will be important in implementing whatever decision you make. In fact, when you search deeper, the other person often comes up with her own answer, which is the right one. And we always work harder on an idea we think is our own!

Skill #4: Seek misunderstanding.

George Bernard Shaw, playwright and cofounder of the London School of Economics, once wrote, "The biggest problem with communication is the illusion that it has taken place."[13] In almost every instance of talking with another person, there will be misunderstanding. To become a lasting leader you have to assume this misunderstanding and seek it out. It also demonstrates that you are really listening and value both the opinion of the person speaking with you and the relationship you two will have going forward.

When your dialogue reaches a decision point, whether in the moment or days later, speak up and say, "I want to clarify what I understand about this issue so there is no miscommunication between us." And then restate the key point and invite your colleague to amend or correct it. The smallest price you will ever pay for correcting miscommunication is right after it occurs!

Ricky Satcher learned the value of keeping communication straight early in his career. Satcher is a market CEO with Health Management Associates. He has been managing hospitals and healthcare facilities for decades. As a market CEO, he has three facilities under his umbrella of responsibility.

Ricky is one of the few clients I have worked with who consistently took responsibility for making sure that his communication with me and my team was clear. Whenever we would need to make an adjustment in a leadership training class or facilitating a management team in solving a problem, he would follow the same path.

That path began with me sitting in his office at the hospital, as I have many times, and listening to him describe a particular problem. Then he would ask for my thoughts. After we had discussed the issues, he would ask me to reflect on them for a few days and then get back with him on my final perspective.

He built in time for a discussion, a review of the discussion, and personal time to reflect and offer a final perspective. Satcher didn't wait for misunderstanding; he assumed it and built a routine to minimize the chance of it happening.

Skill #5: Show appreciation.

It takes courage for an associate to have an honest dialogue with you. From their perspective, and based on your reputation as a listener, it might be quite risky! So, if you would like to see more honest communication, then celebrate it. That's usually the behavior people repeat—namely, the action they are applauded for! This form of appreciation is different from the gift of appreciation (described in detail in chapter 7, "The Gift of Expressing Appreciation for Others' Abilities") that shows others their strengths. This one is simply showing gratitude to your employees for their willingness to share important information or ideas with you.

I am not suggesting a letter or an email but a simple "thank you for talking with me." Preferably say it in person, but if not, over the phone. And it is very important to thank each individual even when you have gained nothing new from the conversation. I wish I could predict which of my employees at what time would have the information I need. I can't do that. If I listen consistently to each of them, however, then I probably won't miss much over time. But if I don't, then I will probably miss a lot and most likely the very thing I needed to hear most!

Consistent listening requires practice. But most of us are looking for a shortcut to success instead of relentless practice. Consequently, our leadership is inconsistent.

It's similar to my golf game. I would rather just go play than spend time working on the practice tee. As a result, I am a high handicapper in golf. That means I don't play very well. I might have a few good shots during a round of golf, and those few are usually the ones I focus on and follow through with. The rest of the time I just wing it!

You can't afford to wing it when listening to your associates. It's not a game. It's real life. Practice these five skills. Celebrate when you get it right and successfully do them. And when you fail, examine what you did. Choose the skill you need to use and keep practicing. Successful leadership is no longer the prize of the smart. It now belongs to those who are willing to do what it takes to bring out the best in the people they lead. When you continually listen to others—your management team, your workforce, your customers— you will gain an understanding that can't be found through independent study or from outside advisors.

RECEIVE THE GIFT OF THANKS IN RETURN.

Valued employees are empowered employees. When you give the gift of listening you send the message that your employees are important to you. And they will react to that in the way they work. Their first reaction is not hesitation, wondering what to do. On the contrary, they will have the confidence to think through the situation, collaborate with another colleague, and then take the action they think is in the best interest of the customer. Can there be any better thank-you to you as a leader than to watch your associates step up and be part of the team?

A lot of leaders give lip service to the notion of "listening to their employees," but when it comes to empowering employees by listening to them, frankly, Sam Walton had few peers. For instance, to inspire his managers to listen he told them, "The key to success is to get into the stores and listen to what the associates have to say. It's terribly important for everyone to get involved. Our best ideas come from clerks and stock boys."[14] They did, and the results of that listening have been astounding.

There is great power in employees who feel strong enough to be independent. When my manager listens to me without prejudice and I feel valued, I will likely choose to model that behavior, listening to others and valuing them. Again, your thank-you for becoming a good listener is employees who will do the same thing and drive the success of your business.

As the CEO and president of General Motors, John F. Smith undertook the most significant reorganization in the company's history. He succeeded in engendering this practice of listening among the management team and the results were that GM went from near bankruptcy to a profit! Smith concluded, "We listened to what our customers wanted and acted on what they said and good things happen to you when you pay attention!"[15]

There is great power in being an informed leader as well. When the company's growth is the result of your listening to those you lead, they will recognize that. They will have a vested interest in your success. They will trust you. Not because you have become one of them; rather, because you have invited them to become more like you—a person who listens with empathy and, as a result, finds understanding.

Understanding is the only path to trust. Trust is the unseen essential that enables work teams to achieve the extraordinary. But trust is also necessary for information to flow freely up and down within an organization. So many of the serious errors that harm our work begin as small issues. Someone notices them, but without an environment that encourages leaders to listen and employees to speak up, those small issues are pushed aside.

Chances are very good that right now your associates have information you need to hear. By choosing to practice all five of the key listening skills we just covered, you will create a new openness to hearing both what needs to be said and what isn't being said. The understanding and resultant trust you gain thereby could make the difference in your career.

CHAPTER 6

THE GIFT OF OFFERING ENCOURAGEMENT TO OTHERS

"I want to *help* you!"

Sometimes the encouragement you need most can come from the place you least expect it. It happened to me when I was in Seattle, Washington, to conduct a workshop for the leaders of the Rockwell Collins Service Center, located just down the road from one of their biggest customers—Boeing.

FIND THE GIFT
it's inside you!

Seattle is an intriguing community. The landscape can be breathtaking even on a rainy day. The sophisticated business environment, from Microsoft to the vibrant entrepreneurial spirit, can be a rush. And the city has passionate sports fans. At the time I was doing consulting work there, everyone was hot for the Mariners and their bigger-than-life manager, Lou Piniella.

As a legendary player with the New York Yankees and then as manager of the World Series champion Cincinnati Reds, Lou made his presence known. But what might have been less known was what a big heart and an encouraging spirit Lou has.

I had begun to realize that personally through the efforts of our mutual friend in Tampa, Monde Flores. Monde and Lou have been close since high school. And Monde, an extremely successful businessman and leader in the local chapter of the Fellowship of Christian Athletes, had invited me to spend time with him and Lou, sharing our faith and growing as husbands, fathers, and businessmen. For almost a year in the 1990s, we met regularly during the off-season and occasionally on the road during the spring and summer.

Monde happened to be in Seattle with Lou while I was there to work with Rockwell. They invited me to lunch and, as I had hoped they would, a night at the King Dome to see the Mariners play. Over lunch Lou asked me about my client in Seattle. At first I froze a bit because, frankly, I was struggling with a lack of confidence and a higher-than-usual level of anxiety about being able to help Rockwell with this particular assignment. (See the box in chapter 8 titled "Make bringing out the best in others your top priority.") I was not as experienced as I needed to be with some of the challenges facing them. Even though I had received strong and positive feedback from my client, I knew that the market forces were formidable. I didn't want to fail them.

Before I could stammer through an answer Lou spoke up: "Rockwell must have a lot of confidence in you." Monde quickly added, "Just think about all the management consultants you flew over between Florida and here—and they chose you!"

Our discussion about this lasted only a few minutes, but those words have remained in my mind and my heart for years. In that moment I found the courage to face my challenge. And that is often how it happens. The slightest thing we can say in a given moment can be the very encouragement someone else needs.

A woman who embodied this truth to the ultimate was the Albanian Catholic nun known affectionately as Mother Teresa. Anyone who spent a moment in her presence found him- or herself encouraged by her faith, her actions, and her words. She once said, "Kind words can be short and easy to speak, but their echoes are truly endless."[1] The power of a leader's words far exceeds the power of the leader's budget. And those words can be simple as long as they inspire courage, confidence, or hope.

Encouragement needs to be served when your employees need it—in the moment. That's why Mother Teresa's comments are so appropriate for work. Encouraging words are usually quick and reflect the need of a particular situation. Connect all of those moments together and you will build a team that can win against any adversity.

> The slightest thing we can say in a given moment can be the very encouragement someone else needs.

Lou also encouraged me with another simple truth. I had asked him what it took to be a successful baseball manager, and he replied, "You have to play today's game, not yesterday's or tomorrow's." How often do you lose a productive day at your job because you are still fretting over an event that happened yesterday or worrying about something you fear will happen tomorrow? Likewise, by intentionally encouraging your employees you can help them stay in their present work rather than still obsessing over a past problem or worrying about a future one.

And for major league baseball managers, this scenario of winning today's game plays out in front of thousands of spectators. When the pitcher gets behind to a batter and there are two men on base, what does the manager do? He calls time and jogs out to the mound.

But does he get up in the pitcher's face and seethe, "You better throw a strike or I'll make sure you're riding a bus in the minors by tomorrow night"? Of course not. The pitcher would either melt in discouragement or stalk off in anger!

Instead he looks at him and says something like: "Remember when you got in this spot last week? You're better than this guy. Throw him a fastball and come back with a change-up and you'll catch him looking."

When one of your employees gets in a jam, what do you do? Immediately step in and encourage her that you have confidence in her abilities?

Or threaten her with her job if she doesn't figure it out? Or, worse yet, try to ignore her and hope it works out?

The poet Ralph Waldo Emerson captured the secret desire of all of us when he wrote, "Our chief want is someone who will inspire us to be what we know we could be."[2] Do you want to be the source of that encouragement to your associates? If you don't then those employees will be tempted to look elsewhere for a leader who lifts them up rather than ignores them. Lasting leaders who develop and retain star performers on their team learn how to bring confidence, courage, and hope to their employees.

> The power of a leader's words far exceeds
> the power of the leader's budget.

Today's uncertain global competitive environment challenges workers every single day, bringing both new obstacles and new opportunities. Knowledge is important, but without the confidence to take a risk, the courage to attempt something new, and the hope that they can succeed, they won't.

Those are the three reasons why an employee needs your encouragement. When the obstacle seems impossible to get over, an employee can lose *confidence* and just do enough to get by. When they are going to have to face a difficult client or a demanding customer, they can lack the *courage* to meet the challenge without giving away too much. And when employees face relentless setbacks—either individually or in their team—they will begin to lose *hope*. This is when a lasting leader steps up with encouraging words.

BUY INTO THE GIFT
it's a matter of choice!

In my early management career, I stepped aside more than I stepped up. Although I knew that becoming an encourager would be important, it took a while before I practiced those behaviors effectively. For example, I would be quick to say something positive to an employee, but it wasn't necessarily encouraging. For instance, I once commented to an assistant, "I know you're trying; just move over and let me do it!" In other words, I was communicating, "Even when you try you can't do it the way I want!"

At other times, my encouragement would be couched in sarcasm, or my words would hint at a threat as much as they would sound encouraging. I usually couched those kind of comments in, "Just wait till I get there; we have to get this right or else!" Remember the letter I received from my associates in Baltimore? It wasn't until then that I took an honest look at how I was communicating and what I was communicating. When I did, I began to realize that I was not inspiring confidence, courage, or hope.

I wanted to solve the problem, but I wanted to do it quickly and with little difficulty for me. Frequently I would take the easiest path so we could just move on. This self-focused thinking kept me from realizing the negative impact the lack of encouragement was having on my employees. Eventually, I reached the conclusion that it was fear that was holding me back from becoming a sincere encourager. What was there to fear, you might ask? I feared losing control. I feared that the employees would take advantage of me. I feared having to fix all of their problems. As a result, what encouragement I gave was connected to what I wanted more than what my associate needed. My staff sensed that and felt manipulated.

In other words, my early attempts at encouragement were more a reflection of my own insecurity than a sincere desire to help an associate grow personally and professionally. That failure to develop an honest interpersonal relationship with the people you lead is the single biggest issue in your leadership. You can't lead from fear!

You'll recall that I mentioned in chapter 3 how influential Nathaniel Branden's writings were to my development as a leader. In his groundbreaking research on self-esteem and work, he drew this conclusion about business managers who attempt to lead from fear: "The higher the self-esteem of the leader, the more likely it is that he or she can perform that function successfully. A mind that distrusts itself cannot inspire the best in the minds of others. Neither can leaders inspire the best in others if their primary need, arising from their own insecurities, is to prove themselves right and others wrong."[3]

In a survey reported in *Business Horizons*, the number-one cause for a manager to fail was "ineffective communication skills and practices," and 78 percent of those surveyed said the second cause was "poor work relationships and interpersonal skills."[4] A wise leader will fear the consequences of not becoming an effective encourager!

The American industrialist Harvey Firestone was passionate about this idea. He frequently reminded his leaders, "It's only as we develop others that we permanently succeed."[5] No one reaches maturity in the workplace without walking through stormy weather, and in order to do so triumphantly, everyone will need encouragement at one time or another. It is precisely when your team is up against a hard deadline or when a customer is upset that your encouraging words make the biggest difference!

But some leaders see "stormy weather" in the office as a reason to lash out and demand better work rather than listening and finding a way to encourage confidence, courage, or hope. This type of leader usually resorts to intimidating associates, firing off a nasty email, or even screaming. In my experience, this harsh communication is more common than many C-suite leaders will admit. And it happens at every leadership level in a company.

In an article titled "Does Yelling Get Results?" the *Wall Street Journal* reported on the effect of a "screaming boss." The conclusion was that few employees do their best work for a demanding, relentless, and discouraging boss. In fact, the results are just the opposite. Citing research from the *Journal of Applied Psychology*, the *WSJ* writer revealed that when bosses yell, employees tend to:

Experience a decrease in working memory (the ability to store and manage information temporarily).

Become less competent in performing tasks.

Quit their jobs at higher rates.

Bring less creativity to their jobs.

Avoid resolving conflicts, allowing them to escalate.

Speed up their work on simple, familiar tasks.[6]

The most significant influence on the kind of "weather" your office personnel experience every day is YOU. As the leader, you set the tone through either your overt expressions or your silence. But make no mistake; the research is compelling that your attitude toward the challenges that are sure to occur will determine whether or not your team excels or retreats.

Some leaders choose to hold their encouragement until after a tough situation has passed. They foolishly think it is better to let associates learn on their own. Would you want hospitals to follow that kind of management practice? On the contrary, encouragement in the midst of a crisis will do more to resolve the situation and strengthen your employee than will hours of praise after the fact.

A popular story is told about Paul "Bear" Bryant, the legendary coach of the University of Alabama football team. A newspaper reporter allegedly asked Bryant if he would ever take advice or encouragement from someone else about how to coach his football team. Bryant was quick to respond. "Of course I will. Anybody in the state of Alabama is free to give me advice. I only have two rules. Rule number 1, you have to give me that advice on a Saturday afternoon between two and four o'clock, and rule number 2, you've got five seconds!" Encouragement works when it is delivered in the midst of the fire. Everybody will know what to do after the fact. It's only encouragement if it arrives when you need it!

How many business meetings do you attend where the topic of discussion is, "What happened?" All the leaders are weighing in on what went wrong and what they believe should have been done differently. Pretty safe discussion isn't it? But what if the majority of our meetings were more in the moment: what are we going to do today about this, and how can we encourage the team to do it? The managers under the influence of fear would be tepid and cautious. But those who had come to believe that their team could be trusted would be quick to want to encourage the team and thus follow their instincts.

Nothing inspires men and women to perform better as a team than the encouraging words of those who lead them. Encouragement breeds confidence, and confidence is the root of all proactive customer-centered action. President James Madison, father of our monetary system, once said, "The circulation of confidence is better than the circulation of money."[7]

As leaders, we cannot always control the circulation of money to our associates, but we do have an unending supply of confidence-building words to spread around, if only we are willing to use them.

WRAP THE GIFT
it's through your encouraging words that you bring hope.

"It's not the load that breaks you down, it's the way you carry it!"[8] That's how Lou Holtz, one of the top three winningest college football coaches of all time, describes a difficult journey. A coach's, or leader's, job is to show the team how to carry the load together. Your encouragement will give hope, and that will lighten the load. Go to www.aleadersgift.com and select the "encouragement" tab to read about how one of our greatest presidents, Abraham Lincoln, received encouragement from the most unusual places and at the most difficult time.

Hope springs! You have heard that phrase before, and it is a notion that has stood the test of time. Solomon, the wise writer of the book of Proverbs in the Old Testament, spoke these words: "Like apples of gold in settings of silver is a word spoken in right circumstances."[9] Solomon just hinted that well thought out words spoken in the right tone and in the right moment were the key to hope. But where does it really come from? After decades of observing, evaluating, and coaching leaders, I am convinced that hope in the workplace springs directly from the leader. And if it doesn't, then rarely will a team achieve their highest potential. As leaders our most potent tool is our tongue.

Barbara Bush didn't spend a lot of time in the workplace, but as a wife and mother she has encouraged a husband and sons who have faced some big odds yet didn't give up. Her advice is pertinent to anyone who is trying to help someone else grow, whether at work or at home; "If human beings are perceived as potential, rather than problems, as possessing strengths instead of weaknesses, as unlimited rather than dull and unresponsive, then they can thrive and grow to their capabilities."[10]

> Encouragement breeds confidence,
> and confidence is the root of all pro-
> active customer-centered leadership.

It may be a simple phrase, a smile, or a pat on the back. But a word of encouragement from you could be the fuel that lights a dream or powers an idea. That's why it's a gift—because so few people are willing to find it, wrap it up, and give it away. Just like the lasting leader's other gifts, of openness, time, and listening, encouragement has to be given freely and without prejudice.

GIVE THE GIFT
it's your actions, not your intentions.

Once you have led people for longer than twenty-four hours you begin to see that hope spawned from encouragement, contrary to what some would want you to believe, is a strategy. It is also a tool and a business resource. An employee can do great work without food or water for several hours, but without hope, even good work is doubtful for longer than a few minutes.

There is a subtle difference between encouragement that works and encouragement that is merely "nice." And that difference is timing. When an associate is obviously in difficulty and you are responding to the obvious, then your words are expected. But when you proactively seek out the one who needs encouragement when it isn't so obvious, then you are building trust.

Why is being proactive so powerful? Tom Peters, in *The Circle of Innovation,* records what Jim O'Toole, the author of *Leading Change,* discovered: "What creates trust, in the end, is the leader's manifest respect for the followers."[11] You have few chances as a leader to show respect for your employees that is more potent than surprising them with words that show you believe they have what it takes to get the job done despite their current challenges.

How do you do it? It begins by dividing your day into three parts for intentional encouragement. Like eating, exercising, or taking your medicine, what gets on your calendar gets done. Here's how I recommend you divide up your workday.

First two hours (7:00 – 9:00): Ask yourself, who needs courage, confidence, or hope that could make a difference in their work today? What have I seen in them in the past that I can use to remind them of their ability? Who could I ask to help them today that would give them hope?

Middle two hours (11:00 – 1:00): Walk around and observe what's happening. Who seems to be stuck? What data have come across my desk this morning that indicate someone has hit a new obstacle? How can I give them hope that we can do this?

Last two hours (4:00 – 6:00): Look around and ask, who is leaving disheartened? Who is staying late or is taking work home? What could I say that would let them know I see the sacrifice they are making and I am willing to help?

You might be thinking, "Barry, you have no idea how busy I get and couldn't possibly find time to do this three times a day!" And you might be right. You are also setting yourself up for mediocrity. Employees who are continuously discouraged or doubtful will stop taking risks. They will hesitate to respond quickly to a customer's request. And, to ease the pain they feel, they will begin to manufacture excuses to explain how "that's just the way it is around here."

The antidote to that kind of thinking is a leader who is engaged, who is proactive about what is going on in the workplace. I have just such a leader in mind.

Justice Anderson is the president of his family's medical product manufacturing and distribution company, Amerx. It would be easy for him to close his door and stay on the phone all day. But because one of the most important things that happens at Amerx is the daily exchange between a doctor's office and an inside customer service representative, his office is positioned so that he can hear the sales team members on their phone calls with those who purchase their products.

He deliberately eavesdrops on their conversations with customers. Why?

He is listening for coaching opportunities. By intentionally paying attention, Anderson can offer encouragement that is born out of a genuine understanding of what is actually happening for his staff. During the day he has brief conversations with the sales team and is able to offer them clear guidance that also encourages them. They *know* he is concerned about what they are actually dealing with, not just looking at the bottom line every day.

Your associates might be spread out, and therefore you may not be able to casually observe what is going on as easily. Some may be on another floor, another city, or even another country! That's why you have to make encouragement a priority. It might mean asking key team members how the day is going and even getting up from behind your desk and going to where they are (or sending a timely email or text). But you cannot afford the luxury of simply waiting for discouragement to become so toxic that it seeps under your door (or through your email inbox)!

Regardless of the business you are in, you are probably hard at work anticipating your customers' or clients' needs. You are convinced that if you can be there first, perhaps even before they realize the need, you will be their supplier of choice or their trusted advisor. Today, that kind of thinking is a competitive advantage.

Wouldn't it make sense to have that competitive advantage with your own team? When they see you approaching their workspace, what do you imagine they are thinking? "Heads up, everybody, the boss is coming!" Or how about, "Oh no, what's she going to find wrong now?" Neither of those thought patterns is very productive and neither indicates a workforce that is genuinely engaged. In fact, it sounds like a leadership environment where the only goal is to catch an associate messing up!

Imagine, on the other hand, your sudden presence being seen as welcomed, with staff saying, "I'm glad she's here; she understands exactly what we're facing." Or how about, "Here comes the boss; he'll help us figure this out." The thoughts that your employees think when you are in their presence will determine how well they will follow your lead. And the best news is this: you get to influence what those thoughts are through the deliberate and consistent actions you take!

Encourage rather than embarrass.

A young mother wanted to encourage her son's piano practice so she took him to a concert featuring the great Polish pianist and composer Ignacy Paderewski. They arrived in the hall early and found their seats. The mother looked down the aisle and spotted on an old friend. Instructing her son to sit still she then walked over to speak to her friend. Within a few moments, however, she began to hear people in the hall murmuring, and when she looked up she saw, to her horror, her young son sitting on the bench in front of the perfectly tuned Steinway. Before she could do anything, he began to pick out the tune "Twinkle, twinkle, little star." From backstage a security guard started to rush toward the stage, but before he could Paderewski himself saw what was happening and quickly ran onstage.

He stood behind the young boy and whispered in his ear, "Don't stop, son; keep playing." With his left hand, the master began to play the bass part, and a moment later he placed his right hand alongside the budding student's and added a running obbligato! The whole time Paderewski kept chanting, "Don't stop, son, don't stop!"

The audience was initially stunned and then burst into spontaneous applause! By not avoiding the difficult situation, the great master placed himself in a vulnerable spot. But he also gave himself the opportunity to prove what his greatness was really made of, namely, humility and a concern for even the youngest student to be encouraged.[13]

If I work for you and I am accustomed to you showing up to encourage me every morning, around noontime, and at the end of the day—looking for some way to give me confidence, courage, or hope—what are my typical thoughts about you going to be? And what kind of loyalty and commitment would those type of thoughts be generating in me?

Einstein said, "In the middle of every difficulty lies opportunity."[12] Your team creates value by overcoming difficulty, and you want to be the leader who believes that in overcoming such difficulty they will also find an opportunity. Give your associates that kind of reputation to live up to and you will have a team that will consistently outperform your expectations.

Every leader will face sudden difficult situations. It might be with a customer or even a disgruntled employee, but it will seem to come out of nowhere, and you can't ignore it. These are the very situations, however, that often reveal the true character of leaders and, if handled well, actually increase their influence with their followers and maybe even their customers. The box on page 102 ("Encourage rather than embarrass") tells a legend about the master pianist Paderewski that demonstrates this truth.

When your team faces a tough situation, what do you do? What do your employees hear from you? Are they confident that no matter how great the difficulty, they can count on you to help them find the courage, the confidence, or the hope to get the job done? If your customers could peek in on you managing your team, would they burst into applause at how well you encourage the team?

An anonymous proverb reads, "Fall down seven times, stand up eight." Let's add to it these words: "Fall down seven times, and your leader will be there to help you stand up eight!" If your team comes to expect that, they will hear your voice of encouragement even when you aren't there.

RECEIVE THE GIFT OF THANKS IN RETURN.

When encouraging your employees becomes a daily routine for you and you are looking for problems your associates might be having so you can help them find courage, confidence, and hope, then you are going to prevent a host of issues. And, even more importantly, you will surpass your customers' every expectation.

That's what Dave Thomas, founder of Wendy's restaurants, found out.

Thomas, who got his start running four Kentucky Fried Chicken franchises, cashed out early and invested his earnings in his own creation. Success came quickly. Too quickly. Thomas would later say that he and the team rested too early on their laurels. "Not looking for a problem is a problem in itself!"[14]

But, to his credit, Thomas made an important change. He began to be proactive in looking for problems in each restaurant because he realized that if his managers didn't take the initiative to look for problems, by the time one was found it might be overwhelming. Thomas developed a process that required managers to call in daily to report on even the smallest of things. He wanted to help every employee find mistakes and correct them, because he believed how you do that makes the man or woman.

A good friend and neighbor of mine, Nick Koulias, has been a Wendy's leader for 25 years, both on the corporate training side and in running franchises. I have watched Nick live out Dave Thomas's admonition about being proactive in finding problems and helping associates improve. And even though he never worked directly for Dave Thomas, Nick has rewarded the company with his own encouragement of Wendy's franchisees and their staffs because that was the culture Wendy's had built.

Near the end of his career, Dave Thomas summed up the key to building a successful business: "A lot of folks don't like routine. Not me. I'm all for it . . . it can cure the most unexpected things."[15]

Encouraging your employees must become routine to you. Your thank-you note will come when you begin to see your employees encouraging each other. Like Dave Thomas, you will have created a culture where no one suffers in silence but everyone steps up to help each other in the light of whatever the challenge is.

Build people and you will be building your own reputation. The reputation you will develop is as a leader who knows how to get business results! Michelle Buck, senior vice president and chief marketing officer of the Hershey Company, summed it up succinctly in an interview with Fawn Germer for her classic *Pearls: Powerful Wisdom from Powerful Women.* "The higher you go in an organization, the more your success is dependent upon the people in your organization. You have to bring out the best in them . . . what you can do to make the biggest impact is hire the right team, get the right people in the right jobs, then motivate and inspire them to bring out the best in them. By connecting with people, you can drive your business results."[16]

Don't miss one of the most crucial moments to connect—when an associate lacks confidence to get the job done, or he doesn't have the courage to take a risk, or he has lost hope and is just trying to get to 5 o'clock. You can't give away enough encouragement at times like that. When the pressure eases or the deadline passes, they will remember how you made them feel long after they have forgotten what you said.

Sometimes what you give away, like encouragement, is exactly what you get back. Another way to say it is this: "Whatever a man sows, he will reap." Let me give you an example that involves Monde Flores and Lou Piniella, who you'll recall from the story I recounted at the opening of this chapter.

My wife and children pulled off a surprise birthday party for me when I reached a milestone (the number is not important!). The room was full of almost 100 friends and clients along with their families. It was embarrassing, humbling, and fun all in the same breath. A few family members and others made some remarks. When Monde stood up, he was very gracious in pointing out how I had been a source of encouragement to both him and Lou. And I remember thinking at that moment how much *they* had encouraged *me*. Not just at lunch that day in Seattle, but in many ways they probably had no idea about.

Lou and Monde valued my input in their lives and their careers, and they expressed that to me. Consequently, that experience helped me build my own confidence in what I was trying to accomplish. And they served as an example to me of how I could be a similar encouragement to other people in my life.

It's a funny thing about encouragement. It's not like a delicate flower you plant and then need to carefully tend to every day. On the contrary, it's more like a dandelion or a wildflower. Once you put out the seed, you can't get rid of it! The more genuine and sincere the encouragement you plant at the very moment people need it, the more it comes back to you in just the right instance.

When you give the gift of encouragement you signal to your team that you value them and that you want them to succeed. And when you consistently encourage others, you create an atmosphere where courage, confidence, and hope flourish like wildflowers. In that environment, goals are exceeded, innovation comes naturally, and personal growth is abundant! Go to www. aleadersgift.com and click on the tab the "Gift of Encouragement" to read real-life examples of workplace encouragement that produced big results.

CHAPTER 7

THE GIFT OF EXPRESSING APPRECIATION FOR OTHERS' ABILITIES

"I want to talk about *your* strengths!"

· ·

Insecure leaders trumpet their authority and use fear to motivate.

The words leaders use to speak to their team, especially the words that show appreciation for their employees' strengths, are like air and water—essential for survival on the job.

When you give away genuine appreciation, it is mirrored back to you in improved attitudes, stronger commitment, and better performance.

Thinking is the fuel of all action. What we think determines our decisions, our deeds, and ultimately our destiny. And what we think more often than not becomes what we say! In fact, our self-talk is so important that we actually measure our mental health by it. When people are consistently negative toward/about themselves, we say that they have "low self-esteem." If their self-talk is grandiose, then we label them as "self-centered" or even narcissistic.

> ## What we think determines our decisions, our deeds, and ultimately our destiny.

When the team you lead sees you coming, how does your presence affect their self-talk? Do they make the immediate assumption that after talking with you they will feel even better about themselves? Or do they fear that speaking with you is going to bring them down or cause them to become discouraged? The words we say to ourselves when we see our boss will determine our ability to follow her as a leader. Our boss's presence will either empower us when they help us see what we do well or it will discourage us when all they do is criticize. Encouragement is giving someone a greater sense of confidence. Showing appreciation for their unique strengths gives someone a greater sense of competence because we have linked their behavior with success in the workplace.

FIND THE GIFT
it's inside you!

The program director at our local radio station was a nice guy, but the only tool he used in managing the staff was to keep a list of every mistake, no matter how small, that you had made. I worked for him part-time, and he always began any conversation we had with, "I have been meaning to mention something to you, Barry . . ." And then he would pour on the criticism. I am sure when the conversation was over he felt relieved and maybe even as though he had accomplished something. But those of us who worked for him felt picked on and demeaned.

William James, the father of American psychology, said, "The deepest principle of human nature is the craving to be appreciated."[1] My boss had no intention of feeding that craving. But if he had, we might have listened to his criticism and improved our work. As it was, we just took our verbal beating and tried to move on. Our number-one goal was to avoid running into him before we left the building at the end of each shift.

It took me a long time to understand this truth about human behavior, but when I finally got it, it changed my relationships with other people. This truth is that every leader has the opportunity to place in every team member's head what they will think to themselves when that leader interacts with them. Will they be thinking that their leader values them? Or will they think their leader is just trying to catch them doing something wrong? And whatever those team members believe the leader thinks about them determines their response to all that the leader asks them to do. This might sound somewhat convoluted, so let me share an exercise I often conduct with my clients to show you what I mean.

Recently, I was working with a group of healthcare professionals, and I was trying to illustrate the power that comes from being an appreciative leader. I wanted them to realize that consistent appreciation of an associate will lead that associate to do all he or she can to live up to our expectations.

My host, Brenda, was a member of the senior management team. I asked the group to listen as I spoke to Brenda and to see if they could identify all of the expressions of appreciation in what I was saying.

I turned to Brenda and began: "Brenda, one of the things I appreciate about you is the way you care about the people you lead. It's a real strength. An example of that is what you said to me on the phone yesterday. You let me know what equipment I would have in the room today for our workshop, and you took a few minutes to let me know what you hoped each participant would gain from our time together. And when I arrived this morning, you were waiting for me to see what I needed. I admire the way you care about the people you lead."

I then asked the group to pinpoint the appreciation I had expressed to Brenda. They all responded quickly: "You described how she prepared you for our meeting today so we would benefit from it." "You're right!" I said. "I told Brenda what I appreciated about her, a strength I had noticed, and then, very importantly, I gave her an example of that so she would be convinced she really was that kind of person." There are two indispensable parts to genuine appreciation: first, a strength you have observed in someone, and second, an example of how you saw her use that strength.

I wanted to drive home this point about how valuable it is for a leader to place true strength-based thoughts into the minds of their associates. "Now imagine if Brenda and I worked together regularly," I added, "and at least once a week I pointed out a strength in her that I appreciated and gave her a specific example of that behavior. Do you think it might positively impact our working relationship?"

Everyone shook their head yes. I then told the group I was going to let them in on the secret to lasting leadership. I then walked over to where Brenda was sitting, pointed politely at her forehead, and said, "A few minutes ago when I was speaking to Brenda it was as though I reached inside her brain and pushed the eject button on the CD audio player that she listens to all day long. And I popped in a CD recording of me pointing out her strength and what I appreciated about her—how she cared for her team and prepared me for today's workshop."

After hesitating for a moment, I looked at each participant and asked a very revealing question. "What do you think the chances are that the next time Brenda and I work together she will replay that CD of what I saw in her and how much I appreciated her willingness to help me make today a success? And isn't it likely when she hears my voice or sees me coming into the room she will remember the strength I saw in her and reach out to help me once again?" I paused, and it was evident by their faces that the group got it. People live up to the expectations of them that we put in their heads to start with!

In other words, people are walking around where you work all day listening to audio files in their heads that have been placed there by other people—and by you. You are no exception; you're scanning your internal audio files even now for an example of what I am saying. Tragically, most of us are playing back conversations like, "Can't you get this right?" "You always get this wrong!" Your employees can't help it. In some cases, the jukebox in their head replays conversations that go back decades!

But here is the amazing truth: we have the ability to put the audio messages into other people's heads that we want them to hear when they see us coming or hear our voice on the phone or see our name on an email. And, over time, they will respond to us in a way that is consistent with what they think about us and what we expect. We really do teach people how to treat us!

Do you remember the acronym we heard when desktop computers first became commonplace? GIGO! It stood for *Garbage in—garbage out!* When we put garbage in our associates' minds, we will get garbage back. But when we put solid example-based truths about their behavior that we want to see more of into their minds, that's what will come out! Do you want a highly productive, self-directed, and responsible workforce? Then what do they need to be thinking about themselves? And, more importantly, what do they believe that you are thinking about them and therefore expect from them?

What follows is a list of three key questions that you must instill positive answers of appreciation to in order to bring out the best in others in your workplace:

1. Does my manager believe I am valuable to her team? Associates who do not believe you value them will become complacent. They will begin to arrive to work as late as possible, do as little as possible, and leave work as soon as possible. On the other hand, valued employees don't want to lose the sense of value they believe that you have for them and will work hard to protect it!

   Jack Welch was famous for his relentless pursuit of improvement, and he would make a point of thanking associates during a plant tour, making sure they knew that he thought they were valued and important to GE's success. When asked about this practice, Welch said, "If you don't do it, you don't have a culture. You are just a bunch of brick and mortar."[2]

2. Does my manager believe I have ideas worth hearing? This is where the gifts of a leader work together in harmony. When you are open to employees and listen to them, you will recognize their strengths and skills that you might otherwise have overlooked!

    In an earlier chapter, I mentioned how much of Wal-Mart's success has come from the good ideas of associates—right down to a guy in the stock room. I have been the lead consultant in more than 400 engagements designed to improve leadership and organizational performance. From companies in the Fortune 100 to small regional family businesses, I have never seen one, not a single one, where the good ideas of the men and women on the front line were not the selfsame ideas that made the biggest difference in terms of customer delight, process improvement, and growth in the bottom line.

3. Does my manager appreciate the contribution I make? How many of your employees walk into your office building thinking, "I hope my contribution today is meaningless!" It's a foolish thought, isn't it? Everyone wants to contribute, and you as their leader are the key to bringing that out.

    John Wooden, the legendary basketball coach at UCLA, realized the power that comes from that discovery. After decades of unprecedented success, he said, "Motivation comes from the belief that ultimate success lies in giving your personal best."[3] Are you the kind of leader who helps associates think that way about themselves? Are you linking what your employees do best with the success factors you are striving for? You are if you choose to become a leader who consistently gives the gift of appreciation.

When everyone else is silent, what do your employees hear? What words do they say to themselves? You have the ability to impact that. But first you have to choose to think differently about what motivates people and the undeniable role you play through the words you speak to them.

BUY INTO THE GIFT
it's a matter of choice!

If what people think determines what they do, why would we ever say things to our employees that would discourage them or bring out the worst in them? It's because we simply don't believe that our words are a powerful motivator in the minds of those who report to us.

Half of the HR managers the Society for Human Resource Management surveyed in 2012 reported that their frontline managers don't show enough appreciation to their associates.[4] And, in my experience, these typical frontline managers explain this by saying, "Their paycheck is my thank-you!" They believe that fear is the best motivator. But that's why typical managers only get typical results! Leaders who make this choice reveal their own sense of insecurity in building strong relationships.

Insecure leaders trumpet their authority and use fear to motivate. If they are breathing they are threatening somebody! This just creates compliance, not competency. Analytical leaders demand exact plans and complete financial projections. They naively believe that anyone can follow a well-written plan. These leaders create dependency, not determination.

Such managers are convinced that fear will cause an employee to get to work on time, focus intently, and perform flawlessly. "Get this project finished on time or there will be consequences!" That's a commonly used veiled threat. But it won't work. When an employee is working out of fear, she will try to do just enough to avoid the potential negative consequences. But an employee who is trying to live up to the good reputation that a leader has painted for her through pointing out her strengths will seek to live up to her leader's expectations. Fear will produce compliance. Appreciation will result in achievement!

Is your goal short term? If so, fear might work to scare everyone into doing his or her best. But if your goal is long-term productivity, fear is the poorest motivator. The Society for Human Resource Management has also been conducting surveys to reveal what motivates employees and what is the most important factor for job satisfaction. Three of the top five drivers of engaged and satisfied employees have to do with their relationship to their manager.

Does my manager utilize my unique skills?

Is there open communication between employees and senior management?

How good is my relationship with my immediate supervisor?

Remember this: The kind of leader you choose to become will determine what kind of team you develop. How will you motivate your associates most effectively?

John Templeton, the founder of the modern-day mutual fund and a titan of leadership, was known for a lifetime of highly ethical behavior and unsurpassed financial success. Since his death the John Templeton Foundation has focused on employee-based research. In a survey of 2,000-plus people, they found that work was the last place people expect to receive a thank-you or any appreciation. Only 10 percent of associates show appreciation to a coworker, and just 8 percent express gratitude to their boss. But more than half of HR managers believe that appreciation cuts down on turnover and 49 percent believe it increases productivity.[5] Despite this compelling evidence, however, leaders still hesitate to show consistent appreciation to their teams.

Why? Because bosses mistakenly fear that too much appreciation will result in employees slacking off or taking advantage of them. Is that your tendency? When someone shows you genuine appreciation, with clear examples of what you have done well, do you tend to take advantage of those people? Of course you don't. It's like those urban myths about a creature that hides in the woods or lurks in the swamp. Fear as an effective motivator is an "office myth." And lasting leaders don't waste time on myths.

But there is subtler fear that many leaders nurture. It goes like this. If I show you appreciation and we develop a better working relationship, then it will be hard for me to discipline you, or worse, have to let you go. I covered this in chapter 3, as you'll recall, in the context of a leader's fear of becoming friends with an associate. But do you want to bet your career on making sure that you have a good environment for firing people!?

It makes more sense to build your career by creating a high-performance work group that will gladly march into the most difficult situation because they believe that you believe in them! Lasting leaders don't wait until a difficult task is complete to say, "I knew you could do it!" Anyone could make that observation after the fact. Lasting leaders place their bet early by pointing out each employee's unique strengths before the job is done and, as a result, ensure that those employees will face their task confidently, knowing that their manager believes in them. And sometimes you have to show that appreciation without the benefit of knowing how the job will turn out.

That happened to me in one of my earliest management consulting engagements. In preparation for a new training exercise, I set up all of the study materials in the studio of a Tampa Bay television station. As the department managers and team leaders began to arrive, I greeted each one and tried to make them feel comfortable. Thankfully, the station president was there to lend an air of importance to the experience. I was used to participants being a bit skeptical at the start of a mandatory training exercise. This one was going to last for months, so I wasn't expecting a lot of initial enthusiasm. But I didn't expect to be met with hostility!

Dan Bradley was the assistant news director. He had cut his journalistic teeth as a photographer, and there wasn't too much mayhem Dan hadn't witnessed. I would soon learn that he was also capable of creating a little mayhem as well! He was the last one to show up in the studio; in fact, I had already begun the orientation. Dan didn't arrive quietly.

Before sitting down, he picked up some of the materials and made a strongly negative remark about them, the class, and me! Everyone in the studio became very quiet, and I could feel the anticipation from the other participants: how are you going to handle this, Mr. Banther? My instinct was to defer to the station president. After all, he had approved this training program and these were his managers. But I knew if I did that I would never build any credibility and the effort would fail.

Leaders have to know how to solve a problem while saving the person involved. I looked at Dan and complimented him on his honesty. "Dan, thanks for being truthful about how you feel. That's a definite strength. I am going to ask you to at least read the introductory material, and if you don't think it is of any value you, don't have to proceed." Dan paused for a moment, looked around the table at his colleagues, and agreed to keep an open mind.

The entire studio let out a sigh of relief. At that moment I was Dan's leader and I had to practice what I was about to teach!

Dan was a man of his word. He read the material and participated fully in the training class. He also began to adjust his management style. He didn't ease off on his high standards and technical expectations for both how a story was written and how it was shot. But he did begin to add appreciation as a tool for building his team. His efforts didn't go unnoticed.

As a result of his growing leadership ability, Dan was promoted to news director and led the station, for the first time in decades, to be rated as the number one news station in the market. And he continued getting better at developing people as much as he did at developing ratings. Within a few years, he was named vice president of news for all the Media General Broadcasting stations.

The words leaders use to speak to their team, especially the words that show appreciation for their employees' strengths, are like air and water—essential for survival on the job. And more than just survival; a leader's words can refresh, strengthen, and nourish team members when they need it most. That's more than money alone could ever do.

WRAP THE GIFT
it's time to bring out the best in your team.

It seems like you can't turn around today without running into mirrors. They're everywhere, especially at work. Haven't you seen them? You have to look closely because they're not obvious. For instance, you walk through the front door at work and the young receptionist doesn't look up to greet you; she's checking her iPhone. She's holding up a mirror that reflects you're not that important to her.

As you walk down the hall to your desk or out onto the shop floor to your station, there are mirrors of opinion everywhere. Some flash back that you're too old. Others say you're the wrong gender. Some suggest you're too tall, others that you're too short. Some read that you're not smart enough for the job anymore and still others suggest you are a know-it-all. Everywhere you turn someone is flashing up an opinion about you, and it's usually less than flattering. It's like being stuck in the house of mirrors at the carnival. Each one is different and just a little less positive than the one before!

When your team passes by you each morning, what reflection do they see of themselves? Are they remembering the harsh words you had for them yesterday? Are they wondering when you are going to speak to them again because you have been distracted lately? Whether you intend to or not, you are holding up a mirror for each of your associates to see their reflection. And the reflection they see determines the words they say to themselves when no one else is speaking.

One of the earliest proponents of appreciation as a leadership skill was Andrew Carnegie, a Scottish-American industrialist who led the growth of the steel industry in the late nineteenth century and became one of America's most successful businessmen and a well-known philanthropist.

Long before any serious research had been done on how appreciation affects working relationships, Carnegie declared that the management of business was actually the management of people. He summed up his philosophy about managing people in a few words. "Labor is never fully paid by money alone . . . you must capture and keep the heart of the original and supremely able man before his brain can do its best."[6]

How does a leader know whether she is committed to holding up a mirror that reflects her team's strengths and examples of where they have excelled? Why not use Carnegie's simple test: Are you engaging the heart of your associates? Or are you so driven by the results that the matters of the heart are only an afterthought when difficulty arises?

If tomorrow you decide to pay someone a compliment at noon every day, you will fail at this gift. If you choose to pay everybody a compliment every day and draw all the attention to yourself, your effort will be seen for what it is—manipulation.

This is a gift that first requires you to take a personal inventory of what matters to you. How important to you are the people you lead? Does it matter to you if they are growing as people because of their association with you? Are you willing to examine the best way each of your associates likes to be shown appreciation and adapt your leadership to fit them? Once you have pondered these questions, you are ready to nurture this gift and begin to give it freely and frequently because then you will be naturally aware of what people are doing right. And the mirror you hold up for them will reflect their strengths, not their flaws.

"You won't worry so much about what people think about you if you realize how little they ever think about you!" my dad used to tell me. The gift of appreciation is not about altering your associates' opinion of you. It's about changing their opinion of themselves.

Think about the team you lead for a moment. If they believed that collectively they had the skills to not only tackle their current work challenges but also to take on new ones without adding more people to the bottom line, would that matter? If your team believed they could handle any customer request without having to engage you because they recognized who among them were brilliant with customers, would that positively affect your performance? This is the job of a leader!

"The best thing a leader can do for a Great Group is to allow its members to discover their own greatness."[7] That's how Warren Bennis and Patricia Biederman described a leader's job in Tom Peters's book, *The Circle of Innovation*. You have a team with greater potential than they realize. It's your job to find their strengths. Discover examples of those and then hold up the mirror until they see in themselves what you see in them! And then it's up to them as a team to maximize their strengths.

Plumbing Distributors Incorporated (PDI) in Atlanta relies primarily on new home construction and home repair. Consequently, the great recession severely hurt their top line and sank many of their competitors. But PDI has been experiencing double-digit growth in their distribution business.

The surprising thing is that when the downturn began in 2008, none of the members of the current executive team was in leadership except Coley Herrin. At that point he was the operations manager, but he would be promoted to general manager and eventually to president. Some had worked at PDI for a long time, and others were new to the team. Herrin is all mirrors! He is constantly holding up the mirror and saying, "Here is the strength I see in you; what are you going to do with it?" Those who chose to believe in what he saw in them have risen to the top. Kenny Rogers, Aimee Gillen, Mildred Puckett, and Jay Wilson liked what they saw in the mirror and stepped up. Today they make up the PDI executive leadership team along with Herrin. And their market growth is just one example of a team, especially a new one, being stronger than any one individual. Go to www.aleadersgift.com to read how, despite facing extraordinary difficulty, the PDI team's common strengths brought them out on top!

Your workplace will never be free from mirrors. But you can, if you choose to become a lasting leader, determine the mirrors that your team sees. And when you intentionally choose to reflect their strengths, an amazing thing happens. They are much quicker to reveal their flaws and work to minimize those. We are drawn to those who bring out the best in us!

GIVE THE GIFT
it's your actions, not your intentions.

Flattery will get you everywhere—everywhere you don't want to go as a leader! Flattery is abhorrent and manipulative. Whether at work or at home, flattering someone borders on being an insult. Now, you may not mean it that way, but that is how it is perceived.

Consider these comments. "Of all the people who work for me, you're one of the best!" "One of the strengths I appreciate about you is the way you

A teacher's gift can last a lifetime.

I still remember the words of appreciation that an unlikely teacher gave me when I probably deserved it the least. As a high school student, I was not good in math or science classes. Clayton Croom taught both chemistry and physics at the small school I went to in the mountains of north Georgia. And even though I had spent a term at Phillips Andover, I still wasn't prepared for Mr. Croom!

As a senior I had to take chemistry in the fall and physics in the spring. In order to go to college, I needed to make more than a passing grade in both. But as the spring semester inched toward graduation, I was in trouble. I began to try to get Mr. Croom to give me some extra credit so I could get over the hump. But, being the dedicated teacher he was, he saw through my motives. He simply admonished me to study harder.

Finally, a few weeks before graduation, Mr. Croom announced an extra credit project. I jumped on it and even finished it early.

The semester ended and I graduated. I also received an envelope from Mr. Croom. But I didn't pay much attention to it until after school was out. When I opened it, I got the surprise of my

thoroughly prepare. Last week when we were getting ready for the audit, you took the time to outline each step."

Which one is flattery and which one is sincere appreciation? The answer is obvious: the first one is flattery. When you flatter someone it only raises more questions, such as what does he want from me? But when you hold up the mirror and say, "I appreciate the way you thoroughly prepare"—and closer still and add, "when we were getting ready for the audit, you took the time to outline each step"—you are giving your associate an example he will remember and try to repeat! Tom Peters puts it this way: "Celebrate the things you want to see more of!"[8]

life. This teacher I had been complaining so much about had written a poem about me!

It's been over four decades since I graduated from high school. I lost the yearbook and my class ring, but I still have that note. It sits on my desk and I read it often.

> An upright gentleman not known to swear,
> you've heard his melodious voice all over the air.
> For his extra-curriculars he's quite renowned,
> A substitute for Barry just won't be found.

I deserved none of that, and yet Mr. Croom had been observing it all. He really couldn't compliment my skills in science but he pointed out my reputation, my work at the radio station, and my involvement in the school.

The poem is merely four lines, yet they have motivated me through countless struggles. This high school teacher with a deep capacity to reach the heart of his students held up a mirror that I could go back to when everything else seemed ugly!

Go to www.aleadersgift.com to read about a conversation I had with Mr. Croom thirty-seven years after he wrote that poem for me.

Words of appreciation that work are those with these two key elements. First, what is the strength you believe your employee is showing? The number of strengths is unlimited: preparation, dedication, attention to detail, enthusiasm, commitment to excellence, care for our customers, etc. The second element is a specific example of that strength at work. That specific example proves to your employee that you have seen that strength and it becomes something she will continue to practice on the job. When your employees see you coming they will repay the strengths and examples you have placed in their mind, and their brain will release a positive reaction to you!

Are words of appreciation really that powerful? In my presentations I say without hesitancy that the closest thing to a "magic bullet" in leadership is this ability to show people what they do well and give those individuals an example that they won't forget.

If you are not sure about the power of appreciation then you are not alone. Oftentimes when I introduce this gift and the idea of becoming an appreciative leader, I get push-back. I was in a Fortune 500 company coaching leaders, for instance, when one of them shouted out, "This is soft stuff; we have a business to run!" Everyone laughed. But I stayed on course and taught them the two elements of appreciation: individual strengths and specific examples of them in the employee's work.

One of the assignments I made was for each participant to take the time over the coming weeks to express their appreciation to at least twenty people they worked with. They rolled their eyes and seemed a bit put off. But when they came back to the class a few weeks later, several of them reported very positive results with those employees they had chosen to appreciate.

Thereafter, every two weeks I held these leaders accountable to find another group of twenty associates and show appreciation to every one of them. Several participants spoke to me privately to report how they were beginning to notice a better relationship with those employees they had begun to show appreciation to. And others even told me they had seen improved performance from several of their employees in just a matter of weeks.

I wasn't surprised. And when you choose to consistently show appreciation that is based on real strengths and behavior, don't think it odd that work productivity picks up. If you continue for at least 30 days to regularly catch your team doing something right, it will no longer be something you *do* but rather the kind of person you are *becoming*—that is, a leader who brings out the best in his or her associates!

My contract with that particular Fortune 500 company ended, and I received good reviews from the participants as to the value of the training. Those reviews are always nice, but what matters most is that months and even years later they continue to demonstrate their new leadership skills consistently.

Several years had passed when I received a letter with the return address of this same company. I opened it up thinking it might be just a form follow-up, but I soon realized it was personal. The writer began by introducing himself as one of the students in my "soft stuff class." He had recently been named the head of his division in this international company. Eager to find out from the selection committee why they chose him (he thought it would be his advanced engineering skill or even his academic research work), he asked, and to his surprise they told him, "Over the past several years, you have gained a reputation for bringing out the best in your people." He ended the letter by writing, "Thank you, Barry. You were right!"

Do you still doubt the power of strength-centered appreciation as a highly effective tool of employee development? Then you would be wrong. Underlying all of this, of course, is a clear understanding of the metrics— the dashboard you follow daily to see if you are on plan and on budget. But when you look to that dashboard first or that is the primary place you look every day, then you will miss the opportunity to build a team that will last long enough to achieve the breakthrough results you have planned for.

When you help your employees believe in their unique strengths you will build the work environment you want. What do they do well? Why do they do that? When they repeat it, what impact does it have on the business? The answers to such questions may indeed be "soft," but that soft stuff is the glue that holds the hard metrics together and gives you a competitive advantage in your marketplace. In fact, the soft stuff is who we really are at work and at home. It's what makes up the unique strengths that form our character. And it is in these unique strengths of your associates that you will discover their core values. And those core values will determine the kind of breakthrough your team will make. Because every employee is functioning from a set of beliefs about themselves that determine their actions.

In order for you to develop your gift of appreciation, I encourage you to follow the seven key steps outlined below. I have taught these steps to thousands of leaders who have told me repeatedly that they work and that they have changed their perspective as a leader.

Make bringing out the best in others your top priority.

I have had dozens of managers try to convince me that the problem with their performance is the failure of their team, not themselves as the manager. That is self-delusion. And it is most tragic when the team is doing pretty well, maybe even hitting revenue or budget goals occasionally, and the manager thinks, "We are doing the best we can." They don't realize that they are settling for much less than they could achieve.

Helping a team achieve more was one of my most challenging consulting engagements. I was retained by Rockwell Collins—the world's leader in avionics and communications—to develop a program that would empower their Service Center employees around the world to be more responsive to each other and, ultimately, to their customers, who happened to be most of the world's leading airlines. I will be very candid with you. I was scared. My expertise was helping leaders communicate better. I didn't know anything about the most sophisticated electronic systems on the planet.

From trains to supersonic aircraft, Rockwell was unsurpassed. The competition kept getting smarter, however, and Rockwell found itself having to pay attention to customers more than ever before. When a component goes bad in the cockpit of a passenger jet it has to be repaired quickly and correctly. The airlines can't wait. Those customers now have choices, and other avionics companies are vying for their attention.

1. Pick up an inexpensive spiral-bound notebook (you can use your phone or computer, but only if it is easily accessible) and label a page for everyone who works for you. (Be prepared that eventually you might even have a separate notebook for each of your direct reports because of the benefits you gain from this practice.)

At first some of Rockwell's leadership team thought training sessions with me were a waste of time. Some even referred to it as "charm school." They questioned investing time and money in anything other than technology training. Since the components they designed for the cockpit that enabled the plane to fly safely were the best in class, what else mattered? Why should they have to work on teamwork and communication?

Mike Maloney was the director of the Rockwell Collins Service Centers worldwide. He made a lasting impression on me when he explained to the naysayers how he was convinced that the future of their industry would demand that employees, even at the technical lead level, would have to believe they were an important part of the entire team. "The more we work on improving our organization's leadership and teamwork skills, the more I realize that these efforts are in support of a journey rather than a destination."

Mike's support gave me the confidence I needed to design a program for Rockwell that was ultimately very successful. The Service Center leaders began putting the development of their employees at the top of their list of priorities. They began to display the same commitment they had always made to technical excellence toward helping associates reach a new level of excellence. They didn't stop striving to achieve all of 't their quality measurements; they just added the human factor.

2. Write down examples of the strengths you see in those associates. Plan to take time daily just for observation and writing these entries.
3. Scan the notebook at least once each week and ask, "Who needs a word of appreciation from me?" Prepare to tell the person the strength and then the specific example of when/where you saw him or her doing this.

4. Scan the notebook at least once each week and ask, "Who needs a written note of appreciation from me?" Prepare to tell the person the strength and then the specific example of when/where you saw him or her doing this. You don't have to wait to express your observation, of course, but if you don't discipline yourself to keep the notebook (like balancing your checkbook) then, you won't do it.

5. Avoid any mention (whether during your conversation or in your written note) of improvements your employees need to make. That is for another time.

6. Be consistent. Don't miss a single day jotting entries in your notebook to use later. And don't miss a single week without someone hearing from you. It takes about twelve weeks before you begin to see a change in both your attitude toward these associates and their performance. Yes, when you start looking for what people do right it will alter your perspective; in other words, you will begin to see the person you were ignoring all along.

7. Take a risk and try this at home. Start keeping a notebook with pages for your spouse, significant other, and children (regardless of their age). At least once a week scan your notes and let one of them know what you have seen, strength and example, and why it is so important to you.

Just think how motivated you would be if your boss managed you by keeping a record of what you do right. Imagine, for example, you are working with your boss in the conference room and she asks you to go to her office to retrieve a file. In glancing over the desk to find the file you see a black notebook with your name on it. You look quickly in both directions and over your shoulder. When you are sure no one is coming, you open the notebook to discover that on every line of every page your boss has written down something you have done well ever since you started working for her. How would you feel about your manager at that moment? One time a member of the audience shouted, "I'd look for the *other* book! There has to be someplace where they are writing down the bad stuff!"

Joking aside, you would feel elated about your boss and your relationship with her. And in all honesty, it would heighten your desire to keep living up to every one of her expectations. That's the power of strength-based motivation.

And there is no place this power can be more evident nor more beneficial than in your home life. We sometimes get fooled into thinking that what our children want and need most is what our money can buy. But, over time, we all come to realize that there is something worth more than money that our parents can give us.

Suppose you have a child graduating from high school (or it could be a niece, nephew, or child of a friend) and you have that special dinner before they go off to college, the military, or to work. You look at them and say, "We wanted to get you a new car but we couldn't quite swing that. But we have a notebook here where each day of your senior year we wrote down three strengths we saw in you, along with examples. When you get out of school, into life, or even after we're gone, open this up and read what we saw in you."

There is nothing, absolutely nothing, you could give a young man or a young woman that would mean more to them decades later. As you read about earlier in this chapter, I know. I see just four lines on a card every day and that poem still inspires me to work hard.

RECEIVE THE GIFT OF THANKS IN RETURN.

I should warn you. The first thank-you you receive for pointing out someone's strengths may be a bit awkward. I know because I have listened as hundreds of leaders have reported to me what happened when they looked at that associate and said, "I appreciate this strength in you and here is an example of it . . ."

Some people to whom you give this gift have never in their life been told by anybody, at work or at home, one thing they have ever done right. They may be stunned silent and some might even tear up. Take that as the most potent thank-you possible. You have just shone a light into a heart that could only sense darkness!

And be prepared for something else. These associates will immediately pay closer attention to their job because there is a chance you might say something like that to them again, and they would get that wonderful feeling all over again. Remember, as human beings we are all drawn to people who bring out the best in us—and tell us about it!

When you write a letter or a note of appreciation, be prepared for it to live on for a long time. Let me give you an example.

When Jack Welch was CEO of General Electric, he would set up a little table in his living room where he sat in the evening and wrote notes to GE employees showing them appreciation. Many times after I share that story at a conference, someone will come up to me and pull out a note he or she got from Jack Welch, holding it like a priceless antique! I once consulted with a man who served as a VP under Welch and asked him about these notes. He looked at me and said without hesitation, do you want to see mine? He hadn't worked for GE in a decade and was now CEO of his own Fortune 500 Company!

What stories will your employees tell about you? When you give away genuine appreciation it is mirrored back to you in improved attitudes, stronger commitment, and better performance. Isn't that what you are supposed to be creating as a leader?

From the start of this book I have told you about my repeated mistake of trying to find a quick gimmick to use to motivate my employees. But when I discovered the gifts that lasting leaders have in common, I realized this was a way of life, not a passing fad. I began my journey to become an appreciative leader decades ago. At first my discipline waned and I would have to get back on track. But after a season, the discipline became a habit and, eventually, the habit became who I am.

I no longer worry too much about what people think about me. My dad was right; they are too busy worrying about themselves. Instead I have tried to focus on holding up the mirror to them in a way that they will see a different side of themselves and a clear example that they really do have strengths. And I have started doing it not just for clients and business associates but for ordinary folks I meet along the way each day.

For example, I once told a hotel clerk in Jacksonville, Florida, that she was excellent at handling disgruntled customers, like the one who had been in front of me. She will not let me forget it. She recently introduced me to her new supervisor and told him that I recognized how good she was with customers. And no matter how long between my visits to that hotel, she goes out of her way to make sure my stay is pleasant.

There is a cherished old nursery rhyme that goes like this,

> One misty, moisty morning,
>
> When cloudy was the weather,
>
> I chanced to meet an old man
>
> Clothed all in leather.
>
> He began to compliment,
>
> And I began to grin—
>
> "How do you do?" and "How do you do?"
>
> And "How do you do?" again![9]

What people do is a result of what they are thinking—both literally and figuratively about the weather. And you can help create their weather! Lasting leaders place the highest value on offering the thoughts for their associates to hear that will compel them to act in a way that brings out their very best. What are your employees thinking about as they approach the workplace each day? Does it bring a smile to their face or a grimace? It's up to you!

CHAPTER 8

A SURE INVESTMENT

. . . .

Some leaders change jobs every three to four years and want you to believe they are climbing the corporate ladder. They swoop in, make some quick changes, and push hard for results. And before it becomes obvious that they are not very good with people, they take flight to their next opportunity. What's actually happening, however, is that they have run out of motivational tricks and cannot generate followers. They don't have the patience to invest in people and develop them. But when a leader chooses to develop the five gifts that lasting leaders have in common, they will foster the kind of workplace that inspires creativity, rewards reasonable risks, and builds confidence in individuals. Their employees will know they are part of a team that respects them. This will happen only as a result of intentional action on your part. Thinking about how you interact with your associates is not enough; you have to be willing to do the hard work and make the investment in others.

LEADERSHIP ISN'T SOMETHING YOU DO; IT'S SOMEONE YOU BECOME.

Lasting leadership comes from a personal transformation, not a personal agenda. The word *transformation* implies a change over a period of time and it suggests a change for the better. Transformation from being a manager to becoming a leader is birthed amid struggles and challenges and, as a result, your influence becomes stronger and more valuable. Some leaders refuse to take any responsibility and others stonewall, waiting for the struggle or challenge to pass. But leaders who are willing to humble themselves and reflect on where they need to grow will be strong enough to stand these inevitable tests.

Transformed leaders bring value to their followers first. They don't put themselves ahead of everyone else. And transformed leaders draw followers by the depth of their character.

Mike Myatt is a contributor to *Forbes* and has boldly proclaimed that "businesses don't fail—leaders do." And the first reason he lists for their failure is "lack of character." He goes on to conclude, "Leaders who fail to demonstrate a constancy of character won't create trust, won't engineer confidence, and won't create loyalty."[1]

Lasting leadership comes from a personal transformation, not a personal agenda.

It takes character to create an environment where associates can help create their future and not be totally dependent upon you as the designated leader.

If you stick around through the difficult times it takes to become a lasting leader, you will have to bring change to your organization. And that means you will have to convince your associates to work with you in bringing about profitable improvement in their work. That's tough to do.

While teaching at Harvard in the '90s, John Kotter produced compelling research that demonstrated that the majority of change programs companies tried to implement failed. McKinsey & Company looked at the topic again in 2008 and concluded that the percentage of change programs that work is still only at about 30 percent.[2] That's why most people would rather move on to another management job than tackle the change necessary to become a lasting leader.

As I examined the lives of lasting leaders, they all seemed to have come through a transformation of who they were. And it began with how they faced tough challenges. Every leader will face obstacles; the real question is, how will they respond? Will the situation transform them into a better leader? Or will the experience leave them bitter?

IT TAKES PATIENCE TO PRODUCE A PROFIT.

When you've earned a return on a financial investment, it probably did not happen by chance, and it certainly did not happen overnight. The same is true with earning the right to be followed by the people who report to you. You earn that right intentionally by how you choose to view them, value them, and align their hopes and dreams with your own.

And once you are in alignment it requires still more time for the leadership relationship to take hold. How long? I have now observed thousands of leaders and what led them to succeed or propelled them to fail. The quickest I have seen a leader gain the trust of a team by truly valuing them was six months. The more common benchmark is one year.

Recently, a client CEO asked my advice on giving a manager another chance at leading. He described the job he was going to offer this employee, and he wanted to give him sixty days to make a difference.

My response was more curt than usual. "Buy a lottery ticket—your odds of success are about the same!" When you place that kind of time limit on new leaders, they will focus squarely on financial goals convinced they don't have time to "get to know" their team. And that's precisely the reason a lot of leaders fail. They are given unrealistic and unworkable deadlines from their boss and then they just pass those on to the people they lead.

I suggested to my client that he tell the new manager he had six months to be able to answer key questions like the ones I listed in the "Find the gift" section of chapter 3, "The Gift of Being Open to Others." He had another three months to align the team according to their skills, unique knowledge, motivations, and so forth. Then, in the three months thereafter, he would begin to assess how well the team would work together. That adds up to a year.

The CEO raised his voice to me and exclaimed, "Banther, I don't have a year to turn this team around!" I asked him how many new managers he had put with this team in the past twelve months and he fired back "Two!" "Well," I replied, "you've already wasted a year because of your impatience."

It takes patience to build relationships, discover people's strengths, help them develop, and build trust. When you achieve those objectives you will have grown out of being a *taker* of time and resources into being a *giver* of openness, time, and appreciation. And all of that comes back to you in the form of a team that believes you have earned the right to lead them. And that team will accomplish more in a shorter period of time than any supposed leader can wrest from subordinates by barking orders!

> It takes patience to build relationships, discover people's strengths, help them develop, and build trust.

The five gifts of a lasting leader express a philosophy about leading people that, if developed within you, will first change the way you think about yourself as a leader and then change the way you think about how you are leading. As a result it will change the way you relate to your employees and associates. When you begin to create openness with your employees, spend time with them, listen to them, encourage them, and appreciate their individual strengths, you will get the performance that has grown an industry leader like Herman Miller (see the box titled "Liberate people to do their best" that follows).

Liberate people to do their best.

Max De Pree's leadership philosophy is simply this: "Liberating people to do what is required of them is the most effective and humane way."[3]

Max should know. His father founded the Herman Miller Company in 1923, naming it after his highly respected father-in-law. When Max took control from his brother in the 1970s, his focus was continuously on human innovation. That focus was so successful at developing and empowering associates that for more than 18 years in a row Herman Miller was named by *Fortune* magazine as one of their "Most Admired" companies. And in the first ten years as its leader, Max led the innovator in contemporary interior furnishings from $49 million in sales to $492 million. No furniture company has had as many designers and as much input on what the individual consumer needs than has Herman Miller. They opened up and they listened to associates, customers, and designers. Consequently, they have not only stayed ahead of the curve on ergonomic design—they have shaped the curve![4]

The work and writing of Max De Pree influenced me during my own leadership transition, especially this quotation: "Whether leaders articulate a personal philosophy or not, their behavior surely expresses a personal set of value and beliefs . . ."[5] I urge you to examine your leadership behavior to see whether it reflects the values and beliefs that you desire and that will work for a lifetime.

LASTING LEADERS DEVELOP THE PEOPLE THEY LEAD WHILE MOVING THEM TOWARD THE GOALS THEY HAVE SET.

When we focus on ourselves as a whole person, we discover that the very leadership skills and qualities we have been looking for are found somewhere very close by. They are not in another MBA or a leadership retreat, however; these qualities are inside us! And they are there in you right now.

For some these qualities are delicate sprouts just waiting to be nurtured, and they will blossom quickly. For others of us they are dormant, trampled underneath years of "the bottom line is the only line" thinking. But they are still there. It took me a long time to discover them, and you'll recall I wrote this book to show you a quicker, more lasting way!

I now know that lasting leaders start with the people they lead first. They develop them and then begin to ramp up their goals. The legendary college football coach Lou Holtz is reported to have told his ragged team of recruits in his first year at Notre Dame that he had one simple goal they would live by. "First we become the best, then we'll become first!"[6]

This book is not about another set of management techniques to trick people into improved performance. You must be genuine in your interest in and the development of your team. I tried the tricks, remember? Sadly, some of them worked in the moment. But it became painfully apparent that I was only showing interest because I wanted something from someone and not because I valued who he was. I was fortunate that many of the employees I was only trying to motivate in the moment appreciated my effort and so we failed together, blissfully!

You are probably grumbling to yourself, "If I get engaged with everyone on my team, when will I have time to get my work done?" But I am convinced, and dozens of clients will attest to this truth, that you must make leading people your first work. Many managers today are working managers, which means they are doing tactical jobs as well as being strategic leaders. The only way to succeed, however, is to develop and enable your team to their highest potential. Otherwise, the tactical work you are doing will be of little importance.

In chapter 6, I introduced you to my colleague and friend Fawn Germer. In her powerful little book *Pearls: Powerful Wisdom from Powerful Women*, she shares part of her interview with Linda Dillman, senior vice president at Hewlett Packard. Dillman captures the key to why developing your team is your "real" work:

> Have the best people working for you. Let your brightest people take leadership roles. My job is to listen and teach—not tell. There is a tendency when you are the leader to think you have to give orders. But if that is what you do, then your organization will only be able

to achieve what you can process. If you teach and enable them to think on their own—and sometimes that means letting them make mistakes—then the results you receive are multifold what they otherwise would be. Plus, it is a lot more fun.[7]

I have now worked with, advised, and observed leaders for over three decades. The ones who last for more than a season are the ones who have focused not on what they do but on who they can become—and that starts with bringing out the best in others. Whether you are in a major corporation or your own small business, today's customer demands require a strong frontline team. As the leader you are the one who must develop, direct, and delegate authority to that team. This is your first work and, if done well, will be your most profitable.

INVESTING IN PEOPLE IS THE RIGHT CHOICE IN ANY ECONOMY.

Every business leader would like to be able to accurately predict the future. Executives want to know just which way the markets will go so they can budget accordingly. Or they want to know what customers will be demanding most and they will focus there. Everyone wants to see growth and profit. After all, those are the goals that matter!

So, can you really afford to keep investing in your employees in a tight economy? Even when the economy is expanding, don't you need to make capital investments first? Shouldn't you pay more attention to the hard costs and then the soft costs of leading a team? These aren't new obstacles, of course, but they can be overwhelming nevertheless. Let me share an example of how to overcome these obstacles that comes from an unlikely source.

Ford Motor Company began the twenty-first century sliding into becoming the nation's number-two automaker. Critics whispered that Ford's product mix was old and they had lost intimacy with their customers. And what no one saw coming was the "great recession" that would cast doubt over even the survival of American automobile manufacturing.

Bill Ford is the great-grandson of Henry Ford and the executive chairman of the board for Ford Motor Company. He was also the CEO, but he made a strategic decision to step aside and bring in a non-automotive leader. He chose to bring in Alan Mulally from Boeing, a successor considerably older than he and who came from a career in aviation.

The new CEO understood commercial airplanes, but what did he know about sedans, coupes, and F-150s? He understood the big issues a manufacturer faces. He knew all about supply chains, lean principles, and customer focus. More importantly, he had also demonstrated an especially strong commitment to the people side of business.

Bill Ford himself has experienced this with his new CEO. "One of the pleasant things that has happened to me is how much I've enjoyed being around him as a person."[8] And this has become evident beyond the boardroom. CNN Money reviewed the company's success despite the drastic economic challenges (and Ford's decision not to take any bailout money from the federal government) and concluded:

> In the course of interviews with employees up and down the ladder at Ford, the picture of success that emerges is one of dedicated employees making thoughtful decisions, allowing the company to find its footing without relying on anything but its own people and principles to get there . . . Ultimately, then, the answer is that it's people, employees at all levels of the company, that made Ford's turnaround a reality.[9]

Time and time again I have seen profound examples of this people-centered leadership in megacorporations and in smaller businesses as well. Many of these, like Ford, are still family-run enterprises.

Regardless of your job title—business owner, president, vice-president, director, or manager—there are some things only you can make the lead investment in. No one can substitute for you and have the same impact. So, wouldn't it make sense to make those tasks your top priority? To take time to understand and listen to the people who do the work?

Lasting leaders pay so much attention to their human "capital" because those people investments are a key reason they consistently outperform the market. (See the box in this section titled "Respected employees create loyal customers.") Jill Coody Smits agrees. She is a Dallas-based journalist who has written effectively about how companies "Cash in on Culture." She concludes that "There's more to a balance sheet than numbers. Happiness counts, too."[10]

Smits reported that a "2011 Gallup poll found that 71% of American employees are disengaged from their workplace, which means their employers will never reap the many benefits of emotionally connected staff members."[11] Disengaged employees can't be led. You have to cajole and push them and hope that they "get it." But a leader who chooses to share the five gifts you've learned more about in the preceding chapters will be able to reengage their team or realize who on their team is not the right fit. Lasting leaders know how to engage an employee or, when necessary, replace them. And those are the two outcomes that are essential in building a successful enterprise.

Respected employees create loyal customers.

As a leader, ask yourself this question: Am I teaching my team how to treat their customers by how I am treating them? I have been the lead consultant on over 400 client engagements, and I have reviewed hundreds of surveys, quality assessments, and case studies. I have never encountered a team of associates who were outperforming their manager's leadership ability. How you treat your associates is a predictor of how they will treat your customers.

Harvard Business Review documented the tangible costs when employees believe they have been treated with disrespect. In a survey of better than 800 managers and workers across seventeen industries, they found that "66% said their performance declined and 25% admitted to taking their frustrations out on customers!" Obviously, this is the polar opposite of the kind of organization a leader is supposed to be trying to produce.

LEADERS WHO SEE THEIR NUMBER-ONE JOB AS BRINGING OUT THE BEST IN PEOPLE CREATE PERSONAL GROWTH, CONFIDENCE, AND LOYALTY.

Leaders make choices every day. They choose what they will focus on and what will get their attention. When you find yourself focusing on the people you lead rather than just tasks to complete, then you have transitioned into making people your priority. This is a subtle but powerful choice that will ultimately determine your chance to succeed.

Leaders who see their number-one job as bringing out the best in those whom they serve, without regard to what it costs them personally, create personal growth and confidence among their employees and loyalty to themselves as the leader.

This is not easy. You are faced every day with work that has to get done. You are probably in an industry where focusing on customers and their expectations consumes most of your energy. But beware the leadership trap that says it makes sense to just focus on customers and please them and everything will work out. Yes, it might—for a little while. But what your customers really need is for *your entire team*, not just you, to have the ability and dedication to serve them.

It's a change in mindset. It's a perspective that says, "I have to choose to put the interests of my team on a par with my own." And by choosing to understand them before you start driving your agenda, you are setting them up for success. And that means your success as a leader!

When you find yourself focusing on the people you lead rather than just tasks to complete, then you have transitioned into making people your priority.

Can you imagine being a leader who puts followers first and enjoying the fruit of that practice for sixty years? I know such a man! His name is Stan Tangalakis, and he is the chairman and CEO of Mercury Medical, a comprehensive healthcare company specializing in anesthesia, respiratory, and critical care products and services. In other words, it is in the business of saving lives every single day.

If you assume that this is a high-pressure industry where it takes the drive and energy of a young man or woman to thrive, then you would be half right. There is a lot of pressure. But Mr. T, as he is affectionately referred to, still succeeds at it Monday through Friday, and I won't tell you how old he is except to say that his 80th birthday was many years ago!

How does he do it? He is consumed with putting others first. Here is an example of how he spends the first half of his typical workday.

> He will start the morning with a bowl of cereal in his office with a few members of his leadership team. But before they get to the business at hand, he wants to know how they are doing. How is their family? He listens with interest and is in no hurry to move on.

> Mid-morning he is on the phone with a field sales manager, listening as she talks about her challenges getting the interest of a purchasing manager from a large hospital. No cajoling. No hammering away with suggestions. Just listening.

> At lunch he is entertaining a possible new employee. Before he ever talks about Mercury, he wants to know all about the employee. What are her hopes? What are her goals? What's important to her family?

Mr. T. has developed the ability to invest 40 to 50 percent of his leadership time not on his company but on the people who do the work. And as a result, they focus the majority of their time on building the business! Go to www.aleadersgift.com and click on Success Stories to read how Mercury Medical used the principles of *A Leader's Gift* to drive growth across their enterprise.

Peter Drucker repeated this simple mantra throughout his six-plus-decades-long career: "What differentiates organizations is whether they can make common people perform uncommon things."[12] That's what makes great leaders. They know how to create influence in peoples' lives so that they can lead them to do extraordinary things. You can be appointed someone's boss but not their leader. Your followers ultimately determine your leadership. That is the first and perhaps most important lesson a young leader must master. You have to earn the respect and influence of those who follow you.

> You can be appointed someone's boss
> but not their leader. Your followers
> ultimately determine your leadership.

Some leaders, like me, take a few years to understand this. And, like me, they have to experience heartache before they finally catch the vision for engaging employees. These days I often advise business leaders that their associates will either be "engaged" or "enraged." How those associates behave rests entirely on what their leader chooses as his or her top priority.

CHAPTER 9

SEEING WHAT NO ONE ELSE SEES

. . . .

What would it mean to you if you knew months ahead of time who on your team was going to achieve their goals and who wasn't? Would it make a difference if your team's individual and collective performances were something you saw coming long before they did? That is one of the additional benefits of exercising the five gifts in your leadership. When you genuinely focus on an individual through the time you spend with them, the way you listen to and encourage them, you will see before they do where there potential lies and where it doesn't.

It's been said that "innovation consists of looking at what everyone else is looking at but seeing what no one else sees."[1] Lasting leaders nurture their ability to see their employees' potential even before those employees do. These five gifts are the platform that the leader then uses to turn potential into performance!

> Lasting leaders nurture their
> ability to see their employees' potential
> even before those employees do.

WHAT CAN YOU EXPECT TO REAP WHEN YOU PRACTICE THESE NEWLY DEVELOPED GIFTS?

When you are regularly encouraging employees and examining their strengths, you will discover what they are best suited for. And if their strengths that you now see don't align with your expectations for the job, then you can either reposition or replace them before it becomes too costly. Most managers I have worked with hesitate to replace team members because they keep "hoping" they will "come around." Stop hoping and know. Invest serious time in an associate's development and you will recognize his potential. Equally important, when you have invested that kind of effort, the employee himself will recognize when he is not the best fit.

Let me illustrate how this works in the real world. A client called me in desperation. "Barry, I have a big problem. Dennis is not getting the job done and I can't put up with it any longer. I need you to help me find an alternative." I didn't say it on the phone but I immediately thought, Dennis is not the root of this problem, and whether or not you can "put up with it" is not the most critical issue.

A few days later I was sitting across from the manager in his office. He thanked me for coming and asked, "What should I do?" I took a deep breath and then responded. "First, let's talk about what you should have done before today. Think back over the past year and tell me about the time you have spent getting to know Dennis, listening to what he is thinking, encouraging him and providing for his incremental development, and appreciating his unique strength."

My client gave me an incredulous look and snapped back, "I don't think you realize how much I have been under the gun to perform, and I haven't had time to hold Dennis's hand!" I didn't blink and quietly replied, "Then you don't have time to be an effective leader. Because had you been doing what I just asked we wouldn't be having this conversation. You would have seen this long before it became a problem. Let me be perfectly honest: you helped create this problem because you ignored your most valuable asset—Dennis."

My client didn't like it one bit, but he stopped and thought about what I had said. He began to realize—as I hope you will, too—that exercising the gifts of lasting leadership allows you to see early on who shouldn't be part of your team. (For more about firing employees, see the box titled "These five gifts create decisive leaders" further on in this section.) Yet it also allows you to develop your team to its fullest. This means you are *developing* talent, not just "looking" for it.

Let me digress for a moment here to discuss the hiring process in general. Most leaders pay attention to job candidates in the application phase, but once the open positions have been filled, those same leaders start looking past the brand-new associates toward their "next hire" or "next opportunity." As a result these managers and executives overlook the potential of a star performer. Oftentimes they let a good employee slip through their fingers only to see them shine somewhere else. And those same leaders often excuse their own poor performance with the common excuse, "Well, hindsight is 20-20." But the future belongs to the leader who sees what everyone else misses in employees and then knows how to develop their raw talent.

Back to my client. I suggested that he take 30 days and intentionally stop blaming Dennis and start being open to understanding who he is and what he is capable of. I advised him to set aside specific time each week to work with Dennis one-on-one and listen to his concerns about the job. To encourage him that the manager genuinely wanted to help him succeed—an element critical to Dennis's receptivity of him as his leader. I encouraged my client to point out Dennis's strengths to him, and to do it quickly. I believed that over the next few weeks either this manager would learn how best to develop Dennis or Dennis would begin to improve because his boss was paying close attention. Either way, my client would solve his problem.

About six weeks later we were back in my client's office to discuss Dennis. But before I could ask the first question, the manager leaned across the desk and said, "This has been an amazing month. I found out that Dennis does have extraordinary execution skills, but he just doesn't have an aptitude for planning. So I assigned the planning piece of his work to Brenda and met with both of them to make sure they knew how to collaborate. Dennis is

These five gifts create decisive leaders.

A wise leader knows the difference between a routine decision and the ones that will alter the course of their career. And a gifted leader will recognize that not making a decision is a decision in itself! One of the toughest lessons I learned as a young business leader was that no one is coming to your rescue. You have to face every moment with a bias toward action rather than procrastination. These gifts don't make you soft and reluctant to make hard decisions. On the contrary, they make you strong and wise enough to face the toughest situations.

Super Bowl–winning coach Tony Dungy has faced a lot of tough decisions both professionally and personally. (And he deserves a lot of credit for the success of the All Pro Dad program I mentioned earlier. He has been the signature supporter of that program.) But he gained his platform of influence by making some tough decisions on the playing field. And those of us who observed him early in his career with the Tampa Bay Bucs could tell he was not an ordinary coach.

From the beginning, Dungy had a calm demeanor both on the sideline and in the locker room. But that didn't mean he was soft or couldn't make a tough decision. On the contrary, he had to cut players he really liked personally and he had to discipline players for their off-the-field antics. In both cases, he chose first to make sure he had gotten to know those players. He spent time with them. He listened to them. He brought out the best in them. Consequently, he was able to make the tough calls when it was necessary to do so. He had earned the right to do that!

happier and his performance is through the roof! And Brenda gets the planning part done smoothly."

When he stopped to take a breath, I asked, "What have you learned from this experience?" He smiled. "I figured you would ask me that. I have learned that I don't have to be the victim of my employees' weaknesses. If I do my job upfront in investing time in them, then I can exploit their strengths and compensate for their weakness." It was my turn to smile, and I said, simply, "Good work."

> The future belongs to the leader
> who sees what everyone else misses
> in employees and then knows how
> to develop their raw talent.

At first glance, it might seem that implementing the principles outlined in *A Leader's Gift* will mean you will constantly be giving to your associates—with no time for yourself. And you will. But an early lesson I heard from my godly grandmother was, "You reap what you sow." I didn't necessarily believe that for a long time. But I can say today with complete confidence that when you lead others by sowing openness, time, listening, encouragement, and appreciation you will reap a harvest far greater than you ever expected!

YOU WILL SEE IN OTHERS WHAT THEY DON'T SEE IN THEMSELVES.

"The most important words you ever hear are the words you say to yourself when no one else is speaking." I am not sure who first said this oft-repeated lore, but I am convinced of the truth it reveals. And I don't want you to overlook this basic building block in becoming an effective leader. What you pay attention to and what you say as a leader affects the people you lead way beyond the issue of the moment. Your actions and words will echo in the minds of your employees when they are alone with their thoughts, and what people think determines what they do! Office rules and policies will never impact behavior as much as how a person thinks. As the leader you have the privilege of influencing that.

Recall from the "Buy into the gift" section of chapter 5 ("The Gift of Listening to Others") that your words—and the actions that support them—are like a mirror that your associates stare into every day. What view of themselves will they see looking back at them? How they answer that question will determine the level of success your team rises to. And that means it's not all about you!

The truth is that selfless leadership is a paradox. The more you focus on your team and developing them than you do focusing on your own immediate interests, the more your success is assured. The more you sacrifice your time and energy to help others see their ability and develop that into a skill, the more they use that skill to support you and your goals. (Read the box titled "What I was teaching other business leaders to do I had to do in my own business!" that follows to see how I learned to practice what I preached.)

EMPLOYEE ENGAGEMENT BEGINS WITH LEADER ENGAGEMENT.

The McNichols Company—the leading distributor of steel products with holes in them (perforated metal, grip strut, wire mesh, etc.)—is a success story of a family-run business on many levels. Bob McNichols founded the company in the 1950s, opening up one small office and a warehouse in Cleveland, Ohio. Tragically Bob was diagnosed with cancer in the 1980s, and his American dream was cut short. Still in his thirties, Bob's son, Gene, took over the role of CEO and continued the expansion his father had planned.

Gene focused on growth and developed a plan to open up distribution centers across the country. But he also made another strategic decision: he chose to invest in the people he had hired. Under his leadership, the McNichols

What I was teaching other business leaders to do I had to do in my own business!

My oldest son, David, grew up working after school and summers in our management consulting business. Before he was a teenager, he was scoring assessments and tabulating employee surveys. And early on he expressed an interest in joining the business.

But I was very clear that he needed to complete his undergraduate degree, to get some experience somewhere else, and to start his graduate work before I would give his request serious consideration. He did each of those, and the time came to bring him on full-time.

In David's first year with us I had a plan in mind for how to develop him and his role in the practice. The only problem is that I didn't clue him in on that! I was way ahead of myself and way out of touch with David's own goals and ability. I wasn't engaging him in his own development. and that meant I was primarily looking at the results, or numbers, I wanted. But people aren't numbers!

The hard truth is that the toughest place to display these skills of developing others according to their own strengths is with the people whom we love the most—our family. And it's not that we don't want the best for them; it's just that we are convinced that we are the ones who know what's best!

That quickly came to a head when David and I were at a conference in Reno, Nevada, where I was presenting and he was there to help me. I was consumed with what I wanted done and gave little regard to his role. We had a "showdown in the desert" over how I wanted something done, without my listening to any input from him. My self-focus sabotaged my leadership, and it produced a conflict between us.

I can now say I am grateful that our time together was difficult because that refocused my attention. Clear as glass, I saw that what I was teaching other business leaders to do I had to do myself in my own business! I discovered that I had to discipline myself even more to earn my son's confidence that I was going to help him develop rather than manipulate him into what I wanted.

So, I opened myself up more to how David saw his career developing, what areas he wanted to focus on. I spent more time with him in unpressured settings having conversations about that. And I had to listen without focusing on my immediate response. That meant I had to encourage him toward his goals and show appreciation for the skills he was building in himself.

I started to realize how important my interaction with him was to his own view of his professional future. And I also realized that the more a leader does this, the less effort you actually have to expend making something happen. David began to take personal responsibility for his own growth.

I saw in him a very strong financial ability and a penchant for details. I could see that he enjoyed managing tactical issues for others and making sure that everything ran efficiently. And all I really had to do now was reflect that viewpoint back to him and encourage him to grow it. (But I still had to resist the temptation to try and tell him exactly what to do.) As a result, he responded more openly to my ideas and offered his own suggestions about how to run our business. In other words, he took ownership!

As I am writing this, David has just been sworn in as a city commissioner in our hometown after a hard-fought election campaign. He continues to run our firm while serving in several civic organizations and community causes. He didn't pursue everything I originally planned for him in the firm, and yet I have gotten everything I hoped for in a business partner in David. There's the paradox! Thankfully I didn't succeed at trying to dictate his work and instead relied on using the leadership gifts I have seen in others to bring out the best in him.

Company was one of the first in their industry to have a company "ambassador" program where they recognized associates for tenure at three, five, ten, and fifteen years. The results speak for themselves: many of those early associates stayed with the company for twenty, twenty-five, and even thirty-plus years.

Gene McNichols is now the CEO and chairman and his son, Scott, is the COO and president. Their number-one concern has always been the development of people first. Products and distribution channels will be the result of a best-in-class "Hole Team" as they affectionately refer to their associates. Scott travels regularly to their branches to listen to the workers, whether it means paying attention to a warehouse steel cutter or making sales calls with a field salesperson halfway across the country.

The result of this investment in the team is more than two decades of strong growth despite economic headwinds and increasing competition. Today the company has eighteen locations from coast to coast. And with more than three-hundred employees spread across the country, it can be cumbersome to provide consistent training. One of the company's key training initiatives is called "Six Pillars." It describes the critical success factors that are absolute if the company is to succeed. I was asked to help plan how McNichols' leadership team would roll out this training.

But before the manager of learning and development and I could make recommendations on how to deliver the program, Scott McNichols made it very clear. He himself would deliver the training to the leadership team and the headquarters personnel. Knowing Scott's style of leadership I wasn't surprised, but frankly, I have never worked with another president who is so willing to become engaged in what he was asking of his associates. No wavering, no delegation, no letting someone else do it.

Scott's commitment to become engaged translated into making some tough choices about what he would have to set aside so he could invest time in the training initiative. He would need to master the material and work on his individual presentation skill; he would, in essence, have to be a transparent example of leading by these Six Pillars. But that is exactly what lasting leaders do: they choose to do those things that only they can do in their business. If the McNichols Company wants every associate to align his or her work with the Six Pillars, only the president can set that tone.

Employee engagement begins with leader engagement.

Scott's attitude reminded me of how Jack Welch personally engaged with every class of management trainees that went through General Electric's world-class management development program. And it's an indicator of a company's chance to succeed.

As a result, I have learned how to predict with great accuracy how engaged a team of managers or associates will be. I simply measure the performance of their leader. How so? Because I have never seen a team rise above the engagement of their leader. If you want to be followed then you have to earn that right by how you engage with your employees and how willing you are to take personal responsibility.

It's been said that managers do things right while leaders do the right thing. That line may be more blurred in the new economy we live in, but one thing remains certain: the greatest competitive advantage of any company, in any industry, remains its people.

A leader's ability to see developing people as his or her greatest responsibility is nonnegotiable today. You simply have to be able to bring out the best in the people you lead and that will require an innovative spirit on your part. But when you do it, and do it consistently, one thing more will also be nonnegotiable, namely, your supreme value to your company. If it's your business then you will benefit for the rest of your life. And if you are a leader in someone else's business you will become his or her greatest asset. Either position is enviable!

Our personal legacy will not be in the things we build or sell. As the ancient writer put it, "Our testimony is not written on tablets of stone but human hearts."[2] The people who live in your wake will define who you are and, eventually, will tell the story of who you were.

CHAPTER 10

LEAVING A LEGACY

. . . .

Every leader leaves a legacy. We just don't always realize it in time to do something about what type it is! But a legacy is not something you are building simply for others to admire. It's the pinnacle of years of work, and the good news is that your legacy is up to you. And the best way to ensure that you leave a tradition of success is to nurture the five gifts that lasting leaders have in common. Looking back on your life is inevitable, but what you see when you look back is a matter of the choices you have made one day at a time.

Every leader leaves a legacy.

There was a time in my life, not very long ago, when my reflection on my life was disappointing. I relived the mistakes I had made as a young leader and even the missteps from a time when I was more mature, yet the results weren't what I had hoped for. And then a wise mentor encouraged me, "Barry, make it your goal to end well." In that moment I stopped being so self-indulgent about my past mistakes and made a slow but deliberate turn away from looking back over my shoulder. Instead, I fixed my attention on becoming a better person in the present. We can't alter our past, but we can shape our future. We *can* end well.

SUCCESSFUL LEADERSHIP IS ROOTED IN HOW WELL YOU DEVELOP OTHERS.

Public sentiment would have us believe that lasting leaders will be known for their big decisions. We tend to think that the heroic acts when we step into the gap for our organizations will define us and our legacy.

But life isn't as simple as just one action. It is more complex than that.

Like the acoustic recording that is actually several tracks overlaying each other, the successful leader spends time over and over again supporting his team. Our legacy is composed of moments that are carefully laid upon each other, not occasional crescendos that grab everyone's attention.

Long-lasting and successful leadership is rooted in how well you develop others. It comes in the normal everyday acts when the chips are down. It happens in the mundane, the times when people don't expect you to step up. The leader who tries to build a legacy on a few big moves in the market will become at best a "one hit wonder." But the leader who patiently develops the five gifts of lasting leadership and makes the choice to put her people first is building a foundation that will outlast even her.

> We can't alter our past, but we can shape our future. We *can* end well.

Consider this example. Chances are you never watched Vince Lombardi coach a football game on television and even less likely that you saw him in person. Yet it is just as likely that you have heard of him and know that he was a highly successful coach. There have been better coaches and coaches who have won more. Why is Lombardi still remembered? Because from the very beginning he believed in building men first, certain that winning would follow. And it did!

"Coaches who can outline plays on a blackboard are a dime a dozen. The ones who win get inside their player and motivate."[1] That sums up Vince

Lombardi's approach. He was a master at instructing players with his transcendent ability to inspire and bring out the best in others. And he saw that as more important than technical expertise. He made it his priority to spend time with his players, getting to know them, encouraging them, appreciating them, and bringing out their best. That became a legacy that has inspired and motivated millions and still outlives him to this day.

Hundreds of miles away from Lombardi's turf in Green Bay, Wisconsin, another man was quietly building his legacy of putting people first and profit second as he began to grow his fast food business in the suburbs of Atlanta, Georgia. His name is Truett Cathy.

After years in the restaurant business, Cathy opened his first Chick-fil-A eatery in 1967. From the start he held on to the principles he learned as a child in Sunday School and from his newspaper route during the Great Depression when he was a teenager. He defined those principles—one of which he called "Put Principles and People Ahead of Profits"[2]—in a five-step recipe for business success. Two of those steps focus on the gifts I have been describing that lasting leaders have in common. Cathy called it "Create a Loyalty Effect."

> Our people are the cornerstone of all that we do at Chick-fil-A. As a chain we believe that attracting great people helps create an unforgettable experience for our customers. It requires a lot of time and effort to make sure you have the right people working the right jobs, but we believe this is time well spent. The bottom line is that our people, from our restaurant Operators to the team members they hire enjoy their work. Fewer than 5% of our franchise Operators leaves the chain in any given year. The more we can foster the feeling that we are a group of people working together, depending on each other, the more likely we are to be loyal to each other.[3]

Remember when I told you earlier about how time spent with your associates not only ensures their growth but also helps you determine who is a good fit? That is the time and effort Cathy is talking about and it is key to the company's leadership development. Ask any Chick-fil-A employee about the company and you will get a similar response: "a great place to work where employees matter." And that is why they have an annual retention rate of better than 94 percent.[4] Chick-fil-A spares no expense in leadership training for its operators, which supports the principle of people ahead of profits.

And it has paid off. From one restaurant in 1967 to more than sixteen-hundred locales today in thirty-eight states! To further demonstrate to his people that they are more important than profits, the restaurants are closed every Sunday so employees can be with their family and, if they choose, worship together.

It has paid off for the communities Chick-fil-A serves as well. Truett Cathy has been involved in supporting foster child needs since his company began, and today his college leadership program not only funds hundreds of scholarships but also is offered on the campus of Berry College in north Georgia. At 92 years of age Truett Cathy has proven that you can build a legacy by putting people first!

Successful leadership is rooted in how well you develop others.

Vince Lombardi and Truett Cathy lived out their investment in people on a national stage. We all benefit from their example. But thousands of other unique leaders who have embraced these 5 gifts of lasting leadership are also building a legacy. I met one of them in a small community on Florida's Gulf Coast. Her name is Kathy Burke.

Like a lot of women with children to raise, Kathy chose nursing as a career. But from the beginning, she had a different viewpoint than most. Kathy learned early on that she could accomplish more through other people than she could by herself. She paid her dues as a staff nurse in surgery, emergency, and intensive care. But it soon became evident to those around her that she had an unusual commitment to helping others succeed right alongside her. As a result she was moved from the bedside to an administrative role.

In 1994 she was named assistant administrator at Charlotte Regional Medical Center in southwest Florida. One of her early associates told me how he noticed she was different right from the start. "Kathy asked questions and then she would be quiet and wait for your answer. I honestly felt like for the first time I was having a conversation with an administrator, not just being told what to do!"

Kathy built her legacy one conversation at a time. I can still recall a conversation she and I had about one of her team members. She patiently told me the challenge she was having, but, unlike many administrators, she didn't stop there. Kathy wanted to know how she could engage this associate and help her improve her performance.

I would continue to work with Kathy for more than a decade as she rose steadily through the ranks from COO to hospital CEO and eventually president overseeing an entire division of hospitals! And each time our conversations revolved around performance. First, how could she improve hers, and second, what could she do to bring out the best in one of her team members.

Kathy's legacy as a leader who could bring out the best in others was not limited to just her immediate employees. She became the CEO of a healthcare system that included two hospitals in the same market. Everyone assumed she would favor one over the other, but Kathy had become so convinced that her people came first that she wasn't looking at two separate units.

She asked me to facilitate a weekend retreat where she would bring together the medical executive teams, the key directors, and the outside community advisory boards from both hospitals. Her assignment to me was clear: "We have to see the value we bring when we work together, not just our individual contributions!" During that weekend I had many casual conversations with the participants. But whether I was speaking with a physician, a director, or a community leader, the conversation was always the same: "Kathy believes in us and what we can accomplish."

Kathy Burke has spent tens of thousands of hours with her associates. She has been open to their ideas; she has invested time in them; she has listened to them; she has encouraged them; and she has shown them appreciation as they all grew as leaders. Her legacy is not in the hospitals she has managed or built but in the people she has graced with her gift of leadership. And she is now the divisional president with responsibility for multiple hospitals.

Recently I was speaking with one of the CEOs who reports to her. I can't tell you how proud I felt for her when, while lamenting the tough challenges facing hospitals today, he said confidently, "Kathy's always got our back!" Every leader leaves a legacy. Kathy Burke realized that in time to do something about it!

THE WAY YOU CONNECT WITH OTHERS IS WHAT REALLY MATTERS.

Retirement parties are very revealing. Despite what we might have spent years focusing on during our careers, the truth seems to come out in these final farewells. Since many of my firm's clients have been with us for a decade or more, I have attended a lot of these events. And I can honestly say that I have *never* heard someone stand up and say, "What I admired most about Ms. Johnson was her ability to balance the books to the penny . . . we're going to miss that." Nor have I heard, "All I want you to know about Mr. Jackson is that he is the smartest manager I have ever had and no one will ever be smarter!"

In fact, the statements I have usually heard reveal just how important the "people connection" really was all along.

> "Larry took the time to get to know me and understand how I learned. And that's why I appreciate the way he managed me."

> "Brenda would come by my cubicle when she knew my work was backed up and she would quietly encourage me to stay focused and just let her know if I needed help. I never did, but just knowing she recognized that made all the difference."

> "Max was the kind of boss that when I had to work with another department he didn't do it for me or make it easy, but he did make sure that the other team knew what we needed and he coached me on how to do it. That meant a lot to me and our success."

Assuming these statements indicate what matters most at the end of a job or even a career, success belongs to the leader who is an influencer and a facilitator. Being smart is no longer enough because we have plenty of "smarts" available on the computer screen in front of us. What we need is a "people manager."

And when you manage people by leading them to discover their own strengths and show them how to use them, those same people will repay you by following you for a long time—maybe even your entire career. These are not just great ideas that sound great in this book. These are real and they are real important!

The notion that effective relationships, especially those between leaders and their associates, are built on something besides numbers is actually wisdom rooted in the beginning of western civilization. In the first century AD there was a Roman city named Philippi that was a retirement haven for Roman soldiers. They could receive a stipend or even land for settling there, but it was a region clearly under Roman rule and domination. There was no free enterprise and slavery was commonplace.

It was into this environment that an ancient writer introduced what at the time was an exceedingly novel idea: showing as much consideration for others as you do yourself is a better way to live. The Apostle Paul was in prison in Rome, but he was able to send a letter to a small band of Christian believers in Philippi that outlined this notion. "Do nothing from selfishness or empty conceit, but with humility of mind regard one another as more important than yourselves; do not merely look out for your own personal interests but also for the interests of others."[5]

When Paul wrote these words there was not a capitalistic economy on the globe, and individual freedoms and liberty were yet to be considered a right of all men. Yet centuries later these ancient words inspired many of the framers of our American independence to propose a society that considers respect and equality a bedrock principle. Because at varying times in history humanity has ignored this truth does not make it any less valid. And today, when respecting the individual is essential, they become words to guide us. If you take the five gifts of a leader—openness, giving time, listening, encouraging, and showing appreciation—they all find a home in these admonitions penned centuries ago.

I am convinced that every human is created with a need to connect meaningfully to another person in an accepting environment. And I am even more persuaded that we naturally respond with greater enthusiasm and trust to leaders who engage with us in a way that respects the unique gifts we have and helps us develop those fully. When you choose to lead this way, you are creating a legacy of people who have lived and worked in your wake and because of that trust are willing to help you tackle infinitely bigger tasks than you would have ever imagined on your own.

And the only price tag for developing people in a way that will allow you to tackle the big opportunity is your willingness to do it. None of these five gifts is accompanied by a requisition slip or a purchase order. Truthfully, I doubt they would even require a budget line in your company. But they do require you to be willing to pay a great price, namely, stop trusting in your own intelligence as your best asset and recognize that it's the people you lead who collectively dwarf any brainpower you bring individually!

Entrepreneurs as well as leaders of nonprofits have demonstrated the power that comes from investing in the people around you. The men and women whose reputation and work has been long lasting are the ones who empowered a team around them.

Next time you are in the break room or a ballroom for a retirement party, listen carefully to what people are saying. How are they remembering the work of the one who is about to leave? Are they talking about how smart she was or how good she was at getting things done through people? And as you leave to go back to your office or drive home, ask yourself "What will they say when my time comes?"

THIS IS THE PATH OF SUCCESSFUL LEADERS.

When I began this journey of trying to fix my own work as a leader, I would never have said there is only one way. There is always more than merely one way to do something, and everyone has to find his or her own path. But after three decades of research, practice, and observation of lasting leaders, I now believe there is truly only one way to build a career as a leader that will last. Even though you may change companies, industries, or professions, the path to success in each of those will still be a result of *how much you pour your life into those you lead.*

This is especially true after you face a setback. If your business fails, the economy pulls the rug out from under you, or you are the victim of inside politics, will you recover? Yes, you will, but only when you begin your next endeavor with the strong belief that it will be more about the people you lead than it will be about you.

Our lives are a mirror of how we have reacted to others in our journey as leaders. Once I understood what these gifts were and how important they were to lasting success, I built them into all of my consulting engagements and every leadership development program we offered. Our firm has completed in excess of four-hundred leadership-consulting engagements, and I have been involved in each of those. I have witnessed firsthand whether or not these five gifts can really make a difference in a leader's career or a business's success. Let me share an example of what can happen.

Paul Catoe was the president and general manager of WFLA-TV in the Tampa Bay market, one of the top fifteen markets in the nation. WFLA had enjoyed a long and strong reputation as a media leader, yet the station's ratings painted a different picture. Why? Inside the station there was growing distrust among the managers, and employees were becoming discouraged.

For almost five years I worked closely with Paul and his team on how to put their emphasis on people to achieve their business goals. It involved individual coaching, management retreats, and developing job-specific leadership initiatives—all centered on the five gifts of a leader and how nurturing those was the key to improving teamwork and leadership.

This effort took time, it took commitment, and it took persistence. But it paid the dividend that Paul and the management team wanted. Here is how Paul summed up the work:

> Our company was in a state of chaos. Departments did not work together, morale was low, and no team spirit existed. In two years [the principles in this book] helped change the culture of our television station. The department walls were torn down, work relationships developed, and pride was restored as we became more customer focused. Barry gave us a sense of purpose and pride about our careers and today we are the number-one rated station in the market.

It works. Leaders who embrace these gifts begin to produce a different kind of associate. They begin, usually very quickly, to build trust and open lines of communication that result in an exchange of information that can radically transform a workplace. The result is enthusiastic followers who sense that they are appreciated.

This further results in employees who are more committed not just to their job but also to the purpose for which their job exists. And if a leader is to move beyond daily firefighting, then that is crucial. Enthusiastic and committed associates become loyal followers, and that is the ultimate definition of a successful leader. Your legacy is no longer what "might have been" but what actually was because of the team your leadership developed. There can be no more significant contribution as a leader.

What kind of leader are you becoming? What are you focused on? Are you still fixed on the numbers first and then, if there is time, you pay attention to the people you lead? Maybe you are already on the same journey as I am to nurture the gifts of openness, giving of your time, listening, encouraging, and appreciating the people in your life at work and at home. Or perhaps you are at the place I was and you are trying to decide if it's worth it. No one can make that decision for you, but a lot of people are depending on you to make the right choice.

On occasion it has crossed my mind what might have happened had I never received the letter from my former employees who challenged my credibility as a leader. Would I have ever realized what it takes to become a lasting leader? Would I have even tried to discover what makes lasting leaders successful? Thankfully, I don't have to answer those questions because I did get the letter, I did stop, alter my course, and over a long period of time find the truth that leadership isn't just about what you do but the kind of person you become.

I now know that the journey to become a lasting leader is never really over. I still look at the numbers in my business every day, but I know that the results ride on the strength of a fully developed team of loyal associates and customers. And that is where I keep my focus.

When we look back on our lives we can see moments that made a profound difference. In hindsight these events look so ordinary that they can almost go unnoticed, yet the choices we make as a result can be life changing. That's what happened to me, and I hope the time we have spent together on these pages has been one of those moments for you.

My life has been greatly blessed by people who were willing to show me a better way, and I have tried to share their wisdom with you. I have also tried to show you where I was off track and how I found a better way to lead and to live. And I am confident these gifts of a lasting leader will work for you just as they have for me and the thousands of leaders who live by them. I am not the leader I set out to become that day in Atlanta, and for that I am grateful.

How about you? Are you satisfied with the results you are getting as a leader? What kind of leader will you be five years from now? How would the people you lead describe you? Have you received your letter yet? Maybe it's yet to come. Maybe it's this book.

THESE GIFTS WORK AT HOME AS WELL AS AT WORK

I turned to my youngest son, 13-year-old John, who was in the passenger seat, and said rather emphatically, "Listen to me, John, this is what you need to do about this and you need to do it today . . ." Before I could finish my task list for him, he shot back, "Don't treat me like a client!" "What do you mean?" I replied. "Just *listen* to me for a minute!" I shut up and I listened, but I honestly didn't hear a lot more of what he said because my mind was racing with the thought of what was wrong. That incident was almost fourteen years ago, but I still clearly remember how I felt.

How did he pick up on my tendency not to listen to clients or employees as well as I should? That began a side trip for me into my home life on this journey to find out what makes some leaders last where others fail. And I quickly came to the conclusion that how we manage the people who work for us and even the clients we serve will be a mirror of how we relate to the people who matter most to us—our family. How much influence do you have with your children? It's up to you. Are you willing to see them as individual people first? More importantly, what kind of legacy are you leaving at home?

My realization as a father that I needed to see each of my sons as an individual and not just someone for me to tell what to do came in the nick of time. At that moment John was fully engaged in playing soccer and baseball. And, frankly, I enjoyed that. I was one of his coaches and I had my own thoughts about what he could achieve on the field. But John was nurturing another interest—music. Earlier as a parent I would have discouraged that but now I knew that I had to be open to his dreams for himself, not mine. I had to display the gifts of a leader at home just like I was beginning to do at work.

On the job I was developing leadership programs around being open toward employees, spending time with associates, listening to them, encouraging them, and appreciating them. But I became convinced that I had to do that as a father as well. In fact, the ultimate test of effective leadership is whether you can do it well on *every* level, not just in one place. A legacy worth leaving is your whole life not just one part of it. How many times have you heard a financially successful businessperson lament his or her failure at home?

So, I encouraged John's journey into music, even if it meant he had to give up competitive sports and I had to become a roadie for his "punk band" (complete with their spray-painted green hair!) on the weekends. I would tell myself, "Stay open Barry; listen, encourage him, and show him his strengths." This was a new me. I wasn't simply focused on what I wanted but the dreams and aspirations both of my sons had for their own lives. The pleasant surprise was that the more I supported their personal goals the more they seemed to listen to my advice!

John's punk phase passed pretty quickly. John became a student at the Tarpon Springs Leadership and Music Conservatory under the influence of one of the best teachers I have ever known, Mr. Kevin Ford. John not only was part of one of the most awarded high school music programs in the country, but also he learned a lot about leadership as well. And so did I.

Using the principles from *A Leader's Gift* as a parent doesn't mean you are hands off. On the contrary, it means you are engaging your son or daughter and trying to help him or her grow and not just become a "mini-me." It means you are open to your child's or your children's dreams for their life; it means that you listen, you encourage, you spend time with them, and you help them see their unique strengths. And when you do those things, disciplining a child is a lot easier—on both of you! For me, switching from being a parent who tried to direct their lives to one who helped my sons discover their strengths and realize their goals meant I got nothing I planned for as a father but everything I hoped for: a relationship with an adult child that was whole. If that is my only legacy it will be enough.

And despite my weak start in helping a young boy become a man, John relentlessly pursued his dream just as his older brother has. Today John is a classical musician who has played with some of the best orchestras in the world. While living and studying in Europe, he became a member of the Amsterdam Brass Quintet. I am grateful that I discovered early the value of bringing out the strengths in him rather than just what I thought was best.

Now, if both of my sons could inject something here they would probably tell you, "Dad doesn't have this down nearly as pat as he is leading you to believe!" And they would be right. But after guiding two sons through adolescence, I can tell you that the gifts of a lasting leader are what you need as a parent also. There still needs to be discipline and clear expectations. But if you are open to who they are (not who you want them to be), if you spend time with them, if you listen to them, if you encourage them, and if you appreciate their strengths and tell them so, you can expect one day to hear them say thank you, despite all the ups and downs along the way!

But parenting is only one part of our life experience. How about your spouse or significant other? How much influence do you have with him or her? I know what you are thinking: how can a book on leadership have anything to do with my partner? Do you remember a phrase I have repeated often in this book: *leadership isn't something you do; it's someone you become*? Just as your children will feel the effect of how you lead at work, so will the man or woman you live with.

If we see our associates as just numbers, an end to a means, it will be hard to turn the switch and see our loved one in a more generous light. My wife, Janice, and I have been married for thirty-seven-plus years, and I am working harder on communication today than ever before! But I can say without a second thought that when I respect her the same way I am suggesting we should respect our employees, life is better! (Just to be safe, I asked her about this sentence and she agreed!) And she has shown me these same gifts in return.

So, why not try being open to your spouse's dreams and goals and not just your plans? Why not try spending more time with her and really listening to what she has to say? Why not encourage him in the areas he is trying to grow and improve in? And why not point out to her specific strengths you see in her and tell her how much you appreciate that? I am not going to say any more about this; just reread this paragraph and try it for thirty days! I think you will be surprised and pleased by what happens!

I have coached and consulted with lots of business leaders who enjoyed great success in the marketplace only to have failed at home. And to some extent that is true of all of us; there are no perfect relationships. But remember what my mentor said that turned me away from self-pity over my leadership shortcomings? "Barry, make your goal to end well." It's not too late to develop the five gifts of a lasting leader and build a relationship with your family members based on that, no matter how old they are or how long it's been since you've tried.

Billionaire philanthropist Ted Turner has written and spoken widely about his tortured relationship with his father. There were beatings and a lot of verbal barrages from his dad. Shortly after his father committed suicide, Turner took over the family's failing advertising business that would be the cornerstone of his worldwide media empire. But despite that success, Turner was still trying to prove something to his dad. Alan Axelrod illustrates that in his book *Profiles in Audacity* when he quotes Turner: "My father died when I was twenty-four and he was the one, really, that I had expected to be the judge of whether I was successful or not."[1]

When Turner appeared on the cover of *Success* magazine, he held it up and said, "Dad, do you see this? I made the cover of *Success* magazine! Is that enough?"[2]

Children often live in the shadow of their parents' legacy long into adulthood. And they often succeed in spite of their parents, but at what price?

When our legacy at work and our legacy at home are built on the same principles of human decency that the five gifts of a lasting leader reflect, then we can expect to be a positive influence on our children and their children for decades. And that is the quiet goal of every mom and dad.

NOTES

. . . .

Chapter 1.
1. Peter Krass, *Book of Leadership Wisdom* (John Wiley & Sons, Inc., 1998), 96
2. Ibid.

Chapter 2.
1. Randy Gage, NSA Central Florida meeting, 2012

Chapter 3.
1. Carl Jung, http://www.Brainyquote.com/quotes/authors/c/carl_jung.html
2. Christine Pornath and Christine Pearson, "The Price of Incivility," *Harvard Business Review* Jan-Feb 2013:117
3. Allison Konrad, "Engaging Employees through High-Involvement Work Practices," *Ivey Business Journal* March/April 2006, http://www.iveybusinessjournal.com/topics/the-workplace/engaging-employees-through-high-involvement-work-practices#UjT6ZCU9KSM
4. Susan M. Heathfield, About.com Guide, "Help People Thrive at Work: Encourage Employee Involvement," http://www.humanresources.about.com/od/success/a/helpthrive.htm
5. Jennifer Reingold, "Southwest's Herb Kelleher: Still crazy after all these years." *Fortune/CNN Money* January 14, 2013, http://management.fortune.cnn.com/2013/01/14/kelleher-southwest-airlines/
6. Ibid.
7. Ralph Waldo Emerson, http://www.Brainyquote.com/quotes/authors/r/ralph-waldo-emerson.html
8. Nathaniel Branden, *Six Pillars of Self Esteem* (Bantam Books, 1994), 259

Chapter 4.
1. Brian Tracy, http://www.FinestQuotes.com/author_quotes-author-Brian Tracy-page-0.html
2. Jane Brody, "Health and the Elderly," *New York Times, Personal Health Section*, January 10, 2012, 1, http://www.nytimes.com/2012/01/10/health/elderly-experts-share-life-advice-in-cornell-project.html

3. Thomas Watson, www.goodreads.com/author/quotes/193655.ThomasWatson

4. Tom Peters, "MBWA after All These Years," http://www.tompeters.com/dispatches/008106.php

5. Mike Hyatt, "Ten Reasons Top Talent Will Leave You," *Forbes,* December 13, 2012, http://www.forbes.com/sites/mikemyatt/2012/12/13/10-reasons-your-top-talent-will-leave-you/Mike Hyatt

6. *1000 CEOs* (DK Publishing, 2009), 120

7. Ibid.

8. Jim Trinka, "What's a Manager To Do?" http://www.fcg.gov/presentationpapers.shtml

9. Ibid.

10. Ibid.

11. Bill Gates, "My Plan to Fix the World's Biggest Problems," *Wall Street Journal* Weekend Edition, January 26-27, 2013, Review Section, Page C1

12. Book of Ephesians 5:15, New Testament, New American Standard Bible (Zondervan, 2002) (NASB)

13. JC Spender and Bruce Strong, "Who Has Innovative Ideas? Employees," http://online.wsj.com/article/SB10001424052748704100604575146083310500518.html

Chapter 5

1. Rogers Commission Report, June 9, 1986, http://www.AerospaceGuide.net/spaceshuttle/challenger_disaster.html

2. Fawn Germer, *Pearls: Powerful Words of Wisdom from Powerful Women* (New House Books, 2012), 150

3. Howick Associates, http://www.listen.org/Resources/Documents/Listening%20Professional%20Volume%203,%20Issue%201.pdf

4. http://www.merriam-webster.com/dictionary/attention

5. Rogers Commission Report, June 9, 1986, http://www.AerospaceGuide.net/spaceshuttle/challenger_disaster.html

6. John Kotter, http://www.LeadersipNow.com/listeningquotes.html

7. Maya Angelou, http://www.GoodReadsQuotes.com/author/quotes/3503.Maya_Angelou

8. Christine Pornath and Christine Pearson, "The Price of Incivility," *Harvard Business Review*, Jan-Feb 2013: 118

9. Scott Peck, http://www.brainyquote.com/quotes/authors/m/m_Scott_Peck.html.

10. Karl Menninger, http://www.BrainyQuote.com/quotes/quotes/k/karlamenn143978.html

11. Peter Drucker, http://www.BrainyQuote.com/quotes/quotes/p/peterdruck142500.html

12. Malcolm Gladwell, http://www.GoodReads.com/quotes/44626-the-key-to-good-decision-making-is-not-knowledge-it

13. George Bernard Shaw, http://www.BrainyQuote.com/quotes/quotes/g/georgebern385438.html

14. Sam Walton, Quotations.about.com/od/stillmorefamouspeople/a/SamWalton1.htm

15. John F. Smith quote on High Gain – The Business of Listening, http://highgain.com/html/listening_quotes_1.html

Chapter 6

1. Mother Theresa, http://www.GoodReads.com/quotes/18064-kind-words-can-be-short-and-easy-to-speak-but

2. Ralph Waldo Emerson, http://www.BrainyQuote.com/quotes/quotes/r/ralphwaldo130588.html
3. Nathaniel Branden, *Six Pillars of Self Esteem* (Bantam, 1994), 257
4. Clinton O. Longnecker, Mitchell Neubert, and Laurence S. Fink, "Causes and Consequences of Managerial Failure in Rapidly Changing Organizations," *Business Horizons*, March-April 2007;50(2): 148-152
5. Harvey Firestone, http://www.BrainyQuote.com/quotes/authors/h/harvey_s_firestone.html
6. Sue Shellenbarger, "When the Boss is a Screamer," *Wall Street Journal*, Personal Journal, August 16, 2012, D1
7. James Madison, http://www.BrainyQuote.com/quotes/quotes/j/jamesmadis399509.html
8. Lou Holtz, http://www.GoodReads.com/ quotes/21657-it-s-not-the-load-that-breaks-you-down-it-s-the-way-you-carry-it
9. Book of Proverbs 25:11, Old Testament, NASB
10. Barbara Bush, http://www.BrainyQuote.com/quotes/authors/b/barbara_bush.html
11. Tom Peters, *The Circle of Innovation* (Knopf, 1997), 141
12. Albert Einstein, http://www.GoodReads.com/quotes/7275-in-the-middle-of-difficulty-lies-opportunity
13. Paderewski, http://www.sermonillustrator.org/illustrator/sermon1a/paderewski.htm (For more information, see http://www.usc.edu/dept/polish_music/news/nov02.html)
14. Krass, *Book of Leadership Wisdom*, 308
15. Ibid.
16. Germer, *Pearls: Powerful Words of Wisdom from Powerful Women*, 166

Chapter 7
1. William James, http://www.BrainyQuote.com/quotes/quotes/w/williamjam125466.html
2. Sue Shellenbarger, "Showing Appreciation at the Office? No, Thanks." *Wall Street Journal*, November 21, 2012, D3
3. John Wooden and Steve Jamison, *My Personal Best* (McGraw-Hill, 2006), 178
4. Shellenbarger, *Wall Street Journal*, D3
5. Ibid.
6. Andrew Carnegie, http://www.brainyquote.com/quotes/quotes/a/andrewcarn130687.html
7. Tom Peters, *The Circle of Innovation* (Knopf, 1997), 145
8. Tom Peters, http://www.brainyquote.com/quotes/quotes/t/tompeters166169.html
9. Poem, http://www.apples4theteacher.com/mother-goose-nursery-rhymes/one-misty-moisty-morning.html

Chapter 8
1. Mike Myatt "Ten Reasons Your Top Talent Will Leave You" *Forbes*, December 13, 2012, http://www.forbes.com/sites/mikemyatt/2012/12/13/10-reasons-your-top-talent-will-leave-you/
2. McKinsey & Company, "Transformational Change," http://www.mckinsey.com/client_service/organization/expertise/transformational_change
3. Krass, *Book of Leadership Wisdom*, 96
4. Ibid.

5. Ibid.
6. Lou Holtz, http://www.teamusa.org/~/media/USA_Volleyball/Documents/Resources/ Sport%20Quotes/ShortQuotes19972010ver31610.pdf
7. Germer, *Pearls: Powerful Wisdom from Powerful Women,* 196
8. Lou Ann Hammond, "How Ford Did It," CNNmoney.com, January 13, 2011 http:// money.cnn.com/2011/01/12/autos/Bill-Ford-Alan-Mulally-carmaker.fortune/index.htm
9. Ibid.
10. Jill Coody Smits, "Cash in on Culture," *Spirit Magazine,* December 2012: 65
11. Ibid., page 65
12. Elizabeth Haas Edersheim, *The Definitive Drucker* (McGraw-Hill, 2007), 162

Chapter 9
1. Albert Szent-Gyorgyi, http://thinkexist.com/quotation/discovery_consists_in_ seeing_what_everyone_else/10155.html
2. 2 Corinthians 3:3, New Testament, NASB

Chapter 10
1. Vince Lombardi, http://www.brainyquote.com/quotes/quotes/v/vincelomba165416.html
2. S. Truett Cathy, TruettCathy.com, CathyFamily.com, http://www.chick-fil-a.com/ Company/Careers-Guide
3. Ibid.
4. Ibid.
5. Book of Philippians 2:3-4, New Testament, NASB

Appendix
1. Alan Axelrod, *Profiles in Audacity: Great Decisions and How They Were Made* (Sterling, 2007), 121
2. Ibid.

Barry Banther frequently delivers keynote addresses and makes presentations at conferences. He shares his lifetime of experience in inspiring, meaningful, and practical ways.

He can be contacted at
Banther Consulting, www.banther.com, 1-800-977-7234.